The
F.A.S.T.R.
Process

The Secret of Emotional Power

Liz Barallon

REDFeather™

MIND | BODY | SPIRIT

4880 Lower Valley Road, Atglen, PA 19310

Other Schiffer Books on Related Subjects:

The Muse in You: Embracing Creativity to Overcome Life's Difficulties
Lynn Newman
ISBN 978-0-7643-5717-6

Get Positive Live Positive: Clearing the Negativity from Your Life
Melinda D. Carver
ISBN 978-0-7643-5291-1

Copyright © 2019 by Liz Barallon

Library of Congress Control Number: 2019934821

Designed by Ashley Millhouse
Cover design by Brenda McCallum
Type set in Helvetica Neue LT Pro/Utopia
ISBN: 978-0-7643-5851-7
Printed in China

Published by Red Feather Mind, Body, Spirit
An imprint of Schiffer Publishing, Ltd.
4880 Lower Valley Road
Atglen, PA 19310
Phone: (610) 593-1777; Fax: (610) 593-2002
E-mail: Info@schifferbooks.com
Web: www.redfeathermbs.com

For our complete selection of fine books on this and related subjects, please visit our website at www.schifferbooks.com. You may also write for a free catalog.

Schiffer Publishing's titles are available at special discounts for bulk purchases for sales promotions or premiums. Special editions, including personalized covers, corporate imprints, and excerpts, can be created in large quantities for special needs. For more information, contact the publisher.

We are always looking for people to write books on new and related subjects. If you have an idea for a book, please contact us at proposals@schifferbooks.com.

*I would like to dedicate this
book to my husband.*

Thank you for providing me with the patience I needed
to get to this point. Your love and support while I found my way
has made me love you even more.

Author Note

This is a work of exploration into nonfiction. Names, characters, places, and incidents are a product of the author's imagination, based on scientific research and ancient text. Any resemblance to actual people, living or dead, or to businesses, companies, events, institutions, or locales is completely coincidental.

This book provides general information, coaching, and discussion about medicine, health, religion, and related subjects. The information is intended to educate, inspire, and hopefully entertain you on your own personal inner-growth journey. The words and other content provided in this book, and in any linked materials, are not intended and should not be construed as medical or religious advice. It is not intended to replace care that is best provided by a qualified health professional, and is not intended as medical advice, diagnosis, or treatment. If the reader or any other person has a medical concern, he or she should consult an appropriately licensed physician or other healthcare worker.

This information is intended to give you the tools to make informed decisions about your lifestyle and health.

If you are under the care of any health professionals, you are strongly encouraged to discuss modifications in your diet, lifestyle, exercise program, nutrition, or use of alternative therapy with them prior to making any changes, and never discontinue or reduce prescription medications without consulting your doctor or pharmacist.

CONTENTS

Special Thanks

Thank you to my friends and clients for providing their life situations for me to help them with. This allowed me the ability to develop this F.A.S.T.R. Process, meaning that I could teach others how to overcome their emotional pain in a healthy way.

Thank you to my amazing parents. You brought me up in a loving environment that allowed me to explore my own emotions in a healthy way. This paved the way for me to observe a cultural deficiency in comparison to my own upbringing. And thank you to my children. Through your eyes, I saw the capability of a world worthy of your future adventures. Through your eyes and your words, I found the magic of the truth of love within.

INTRODUCTION

Once upon a time there was a person who wanted to make a difference.
This person lived in a comfortable house and had a comfortable life.
But it wasn't enough.
There was a hole in their heart that longed for more.
But it seemed that no matter how hard they tried,
they just kept ending up back where they started.
They followed this advice and they followed that advice.
But nothing seemed to work!
They didn't realize that one thing was missing—
something that they had overlooked for many years,
something that worked like magic
to create the reality of their dreams.
So they too could live happily ever after!

The F.A.S.T.R. Process shares the secret to attain the outcome you desire simply by focusing on the one thing we often overlook in life. Our emotions. The F.A.S.T.R. Process will teach you how to master the art of guiding your emotions to the point where you can overcome any obstacle easily and in turn learn through balance and intention that you have the power to attract anything you desire.

Are you ready to learn the secret of the F.A.S.T.R. Process?

What if your rock bottom was
actually your foundation to
build your true home?

— LIZ BARALLON —

Chapter 1
THE POWER OF FALLING

Rock Bottom and I have been intimately acquainted many times over the past. Just as I'm sure you know Rock Bottom all too well. My story isn't any more special or worse than yours. It's simply *my* story. It's my road I chose to travel, and it's my journey in this wonderful thing we call life. Fifteen years ago, my most devastating rock bottom came to eat me up so much that I devastated many relationships, both friendship and romantic, and during the next tumultuous eight years, I transitioned through depression, sadness, betrayal, and hurt. I'm sure you can imagine that I was lower than low.

I blamed everyone. I blamed women, I blamed men, I blamed the internet, I blamed myself, I blamed my boyfriend, I blamed my family, I blamed my circumstances.

I grieved, I cried, I fell silent, I hated, I retreated, I got angry, I was regretful, and I vowed I would get even.

A shattered heart is probably the worst thing you could ever go through emotionally—culminating in breaking you down to your lowest level. You become so numb you can't think, and you can't even trust what you are thinking. Your emotions jump all over the place, ranging from grief to relief, then back to sadness and pain, before finally cracking a little to let in a glimmer of hope. Then your emotions plummet again to start all over. But mostly you feel broken. You are so broken that your very core dims; your heart sinks you into the ground, and you simply cannot fathom life any further. You have no choice but to go back to basics, and put one foot in front of the other to take each second as it comes.

For me, I literally felt my Higher Self take over. It felt like my mind had shut off and my body was on vital function only. I was surviving on little food and not much else. Just opening my eyes in the morning hurt. They were usually welded shut by my tears throughout the night. In that dark time of my life, my Spirit was the one that came in and took over the operating system. I don't even remember much, and it feels quite murky and foggy when I try to think back to it. All I remember was feeling completely shattered. Not only my heart but also my *Whole Self* (body, mind, and spirit) had separated, and I no longer felt connected or *whole*.

This is a story about reconnection with your Higher Self. It is a story about realizing the truth of life itself. It is a story about finding the light through the fog and seeing things as they really are. It is a story about all the things I have learned, studied, and developed over the last nine years. And it is about my five-step process to help you overcome fear, pain, confusion, guilt, anger, hate, judgment, and anything else holding you back from finding your true light, and becoming the person you are destined to become through realizing your true divine purpose.

Maybe, just like me, your rock bottom is your foundation to build your new home more "holistically." Maybe, just like me, your rock bottom is telling you, "I don't belong here anymore." Here's what I can tell you for sure. You can either sink, change, or grow, but I know that simply by the process of you choosing this book that now is *your* time to let the light in and start to shine again.

All your life you have been told things like: "Big boys don't cry," "Kids should be seen and not heard," ""Suck it up," "Toughen up," "Get over it," or "Build a bridge." The unfortunate thing is that I could keep going with these sayings we have all heard since we were kids. Is it any wonder we are all emotionally inept? You have been taught since you were young to suppress your feelings, to hide your thoughts, and to keep your opinions to yourself. Who taught you the correct way to deal with your emotions? Don't you just hide them away, pretend they aren't happening, and feel guilty for even being sad?

And then someone asks you to be an adult! They ask you how you are feeling, why you are feeling it, and why can't you stop feeling it. You know what I mean, right? Nobody taught you these things, but then you are expected to just *know* how to deal with it.

Your Fear to talk about your emotions has stemmed from a silenced upbringing, and I'm sure you all still feel the guilt of having any kind of negative feelings. Those pesky, weak emotions, right? Well, no more!

I'm going to turn your guilt for feeling sad, angry, fearful, or whatever negative emotion you have, on its head.

I'm about to teach you my pioneered five-step method to look at any emotional pain and take it from its negative vibrations to a more positive vibration very quickly. And it's all about the realization of the pain being there in the first place and then gaining the *intent* to heal completely.

My revolutionary process is called the F.A.S.T.R. Process.

Over the coming chapters you will be learning about:

F eel
A cknowledge
S tart
T hank
R elease

STEP ONE:

Feel

Chapter 2
THE POWER OF YOUR EMOTIONAL PAIN

Pain is very important to feel. These emotions of grief, anger, frustration, hurt, and betrayal are horrible, but they are important. As human beings, we have the right to experience all facets of emotion. I believe that for you to evolve to your highest version of you, and to truly find your divine purpose, you need to feel this pain completely. You need to fall before you can fly. You need to know what this pain feels like, and you need to know that without a doubt, you never want to be here in this darkness again. This pain is your signal to aim for better. Without this pain and this hurt, you cannot know what it is you *don't* want, and you cannot determine what it is that you *do* want. However, even though I say you must allow yourself to feel the pain, it is important, and in fact vital, for you not to get lost in it.

Everybody has his or her own version of pain. No two people will ever experience the exact same pain. Of course you can go through the same experience as someone else, but your individual upbringing, thoughts, and emotions will take that situation and create your pain individually. The only thing you can control is your own reaction to the situation, and this involves learning and knowing what you can do to turn it around and how you can overcome the obstacle. Don't let this pain alone ruin relationships or tear families or friendships apart. Don't let that pain control you. Don't let the pain *become* you. You are not the pain!

Hitting rock bottom is a very traumatic time in your life. At the time it feels like no one else could possibly know how bad you are feeling. How could anyone else have felt this bad and brokenhearted ever? Your body gets heavy and you lose interest in everything. You either cry an ocean or you become like a stone frozen in shock. Sometimes you just swap between the two.

The ability to make decisions disappears, and if someone else relies on you, you switch onto autopilot in a fog with no memory of anything five minutes prior. Your body reverts back to basics, and you do your very best just to minimally function. Rock bottom is usually a gut-wrenching experience of facing your own self-worth. It's a feeling of not being good enough, and it can smash your heart into the ground. It literally feels like your heart is shattered. How could you ever repair it?

Unfortunately, you will never truly repair a shattered heart. No matter how hard you try, the cracks will always be there. However, I can tell you right now that you may never actually want to. Did you know that, in Japan, when a beautiful piece of crockery shatters, they repair it with gold, because they believe that the crack is a unique piece of the object's history that only adds to its beauty? Your heart can be mended with gold, but the flaws will always be there. These are the flaws that only serve to make you stronger, more beautiful, and, most importantly, to start you on the journey to ascending into your own divine purpose.

Striving for your goals or your divine purpose in life can be a monumental task. To some people this drive comes naturally, but to others they get lost along the way. They may take tangents, or stop at a crossroads, or even stand still in the dark out of fear of the unknown.

You see, fear is a funny thing. We feel fear to help keep us safe. It can be a good thing when it comes to life or death situations; however, when it comes to achieving a goal or a life purpose, fear can be your worst enemy.

Have you seen *Rise of the Guardians*? It's a great kids' movie about a child's natural inclination and ability to believe in magic! It features Santa, the Easter Bunny, the Tooth Fairy, the Sandman, and the unlikely character of Jack Frost. The Moon has chosen these characters to be the guardians of the world, but the story must also feature the opposing force, and that comes in the form of Pitch Black, the Bogeyman. The story focuses on the beliefs of children from around the world. When a child believes in one of the characters, they have the ability to see that character, and that character remains in our reality. The major story line focuses on the troubles of the forgotten Jack Frost, who remains invisible to everyone except one little boy who does still believe in him. Jack then takes that child's belief in him and turns it into his own realization for his incredible potential to go on to save the world from the Bogeyman, who is trying to take over the world with the power of fear.

There are amazing parallels in this movie to our real-life everyday troubles. Imagine the world in this scenario as your whole bodily entity. The Bogeyman represents fear and pain in your life. He lives and thrives off the fear in your mind, and he grows bigger as more and more fear increases throughout your world. He wants your whole being to fear him, because this gives him more power, allowing him to rule your world. In the process of world domination, the Bogeyman injures the Sandman, who is the maker of your dreams. So this means that Fear kills Dreams. Look at the truth in that! Jack Frost, on the other hand, represents your inner self-worth. He thinks he is invisible to all and has become consumed with his self-worth obsession, or lack thereof. This dim view of himself caused Jack to misbehave throughout your world, until the Moon calls on him one day to become a guardian to protect the world from the Bogeyman. The Moon represents the light of the truth. That light shines through and ventures down to every single one of us when we are in a dark place, and tells us to get back up, because we have a purpose in life to become more than someone who is simply consumed in the darkness of fear. It is the truth that self-love is within and that truth is handed to Jack through a small boy, who says to Jack, "I see you." This self-love allows you to see your self-worth. And this sense of feeling worthy to at least one person makes Jack reflect within, to then demonstrate the amazing power of self-discovery and overcome his own fears and emotional darkness to succeed, to bring back dreams (the Sandman) and then squash fear (the Bogeyman).

Like the small boy in the movie, here I stand saying, "I see you."

You are worthy! You are brave! You've decided to take on this journey of emotional elevation. That takes courage and strength and trust.

Being locked into fear can be described as quite painful. For example, stress is defined as "a state of mental or emotional strain or tension resulting from adverse or demanding circumstances," and anxiety is defined as "a feeling of worry, nervousness, or unease about something with an uncertain outcome." This equates to simply "fear of the unknown."

Usually, stress and anxiety go hand in hand, and it is the emotion of *fear* that controls both stress and anxiety. It is the fear of the unknown that can cause the underlying worry, keeping your mind focused on fear alone. This is one of the main causes underlying stress and anxiety. Your mind, or your ego, is what allows that fear to be the dominant emotion. And it is your ego that allows you to stay comfortable in your circle of "what is known" and to stay right where you are. At least you know this pain and you know that you can work around it, right? After all, you have been doing it for so long! It's like the white elephant in the room. You know it's there; you just think you can ignore it and still live happily while not pushing yourself to do anything you dream of, but unfortunately, unless you acknowledge the white elephant, it will always be there unconsciously reminding you that there is something more to life.

The only way to conquer stress and anxiety is to take back the control of your thoughts and balance your ego. To do this you need to learn how to recognize when your thoughts are being controlled by your emotions, and then learn what you need to do to turn it around so it is finally your thoughts that guide your emotions, and that, ultimately, they are working together in a balanced harmony.

Many scholars will suggest that you face your fear, or say a mantra, or change your thoughts around, but there aren't many out there who will give you the reasons behind why you should do this, or the practical tools you need to do this. Just the fear of facing a fear is enough to send most people running, especially if they haven't sat down to focus on the dream that they so desperately want to achieve. It is far easier to put the dream out of your mind and think, "maybe one day," knowing full well that the aforementioned day will probably never come, than it is to bring the dream to the forefront of your mind in order to pursue it.

This book will help you understand why not just *fear* but *emotions* in general are so important, and what steps you can take to face those fears and achieve your dreams.

What is your "one day when"? Can you think of that thing that you want to do one day, when you have enough money? One day when things get a little less chaotic? One day when the kids are at school? One day when the kids are out of school? One day when you have some time to sit down? What is that one thing you keep putting off that you think will make you successful?

I'm sorry to be the bearer of bad news, but unless you win the lottery, that day will never come. Life always has obstacles, and our brain is quite happy to oblige those obstacles. However, doing that "one day when" might actually make you stretch yourself and face your fear head on. It will come with feelings of being uncomfortable, stressed, or anxious. But your "one day when" should be a goal or dream big enough to make those feelings worth it. When you get to the end of your life, will not doing that "one day when" be far worse?

Nothing worth fighting for is ever easy, and as Alfred Tennyson said, "It is better to have tried and failed than to live a life wondering what would've happened if I had tried."

Taking that big goal—that "one day when"—is a great way to set a determination to force yourself to face fear.

Did you know that when successful people are asked how they became so successful, they didn't say, "Well, I waited for the time to be right, and I then nutted out my business plan, and strategized over it for two years, and spoke to many people to see what they thought of my idea." No they didn't do that at all. They said, "I can do this," jumped right it, and figured out the plan as they went along. Richard Branson was in debt for the first fifteen years of his business life. Sure, many successful people have failed. Many of them failed many times. But the difference lies in the getting back up—the learning they took away from each failure, and their ability to improve each time.

The only way to learn and grow and become a better person is to make mistakes. If you fear making mistakes, then you are limiting your inner growth. So this is where you now realize that the really successful people in life actually love making mistakes. They love getting criticism; they love hearing "You can't do that!" Why? Because it allows them to grow, improve, and succeed, where others gave up. Instead of hanging their head low in shame, they ask, "Oh? Why do you think I can't do that?" They listen to the criticism and work out a way to overcome it. They can then implement it into their business, or their attitude, and all of a sudden, they are improving.

As I've mentioned earlier, as children, we were programmed to hide our emotions. "Big boys don't cry." "Kids should be seen and not heard." It took courage back then to hide our crying, to stifle our tears, to find a pillow to cry into. We had to face these feelings alone because our parents didn't know how to deal with it, or maybe they didn't even *want* to deal with it. We were taught to be brave and not feel. We were taught that feeling sad wasn't acceptable. And that "weak emotions" should be drilled out of us. That's not our parents' fault. Unfortunately, it is ingrained into all generations as children and then further ingrained into us through school, media, and governments. We no longer know how to process these emotions in a healthy way. We hide true feelings or blurt them out angrily, usually thinking we are doing the right thing either way. All it has accomplished is the production of generations of people hiding in the darkness of their sadness and not facing their fears.

Hiding your feelings to not hurt others' feelings is brave because it takes a lot of effort and goes against all your natural instincts. But learning to deal with these emotions in a healthy way is much braver.

Now that I have spoken about the emotion of fear controlling far too many people, I will tell you now that fear or pain is actually not evil. In fact, feeling emotional pain of any sort is a vital part of your journey. Without pain, we cannot know true happiness. As we all know, fear helps trigger the flight, fight, or freeze response. Back when humans were hunter-gatherers, this response was a vital part of survival, and now, scarily similar in our technologically advanced society, it still seems to be vital for a different type of survival. These days, humans mainly apply fear to remaining in simple survival mode. The stresses of everyday survival to stay in the rat race, to earn the money, and to pay the bills for the things we perceive as essential for our comfort place us firmly on autopilot. Staying safe (flight or freeze). So Fear equals "keep me safe" in the brain. Or these days it means "Keep me from being on the streets and starving." Fear is *your security blanket.*

However, back in the hunter-gatherer days, humanity still needed people to fight. Humanity still needed people who would take their fear and go out and kill the threat to keep others safe. Now, it is still the same. We still need people who will fight for their dreams. We still need people who will go out and smash the threat of the fear and succeed to make the world a safer and better place.

If you stay in your hut and wait out the threat, you will never know if that threat is truly gone. You won't ever venture beyond the confines of your hut. You won't ever see the gorgeous blue sky. You won't ever smell the aromatic flowers. You won't ever see a sunrise or a sunset. You won't ever realize what other wonderful things exist, through staying put.

The word "emotion" is derived from the Old French root word *emouvoir*, meaning to "stir up," and from the Latin *emovere*, meaning to "move out, remove, or agitate."

Maybe it just so happens that your emotions are happening for a reason. Your emotions occur to help you move, stir yourself up, and grow.

Let's strip it right back to our basics and look at our blood cells. Our red blood cells are the workers. They carry the oxygen and vital nutrients around our body, working day in and day out, just doing their job. Then we have the white blood cells. They are much less in number, but they are the ones that face the fear to go and fight the invaders of viruses, fungi, and bacteria. They are so clever too, because they need to analyze each and every threat to determine the best way to fight it, and then they learn from that experience so that the next time that same infection enters into the body, those white cells pull out the memory of what worked best last time, and that threat is eliminated immediately.

Do you want to be the red blood cell or the white blood cell?

Feeling fear is of course important, but so is realizing that it isn't limiting. When you think of the feeling of fear, do you get a good feeling in your gut, or do you get a bad feeling in your gut? That bad feeling is a signal to your body to *move*. Not just physically, but mentally as well, depending on the situation. Your fear or hurt is only the instigator of your strength. It is your springboard to happiness! Hurt can take many forms: sadness, feeling down, boredom, anxiousness, anger, stress, fear, or emptiness, and as annoying or painful as these feelings are, they are messages to you that you are not getting something you need. It is your Higher Self telling you that there is more to learn and conquer.

Our Whole Self is made of three vital parts: your Body, your Mind, and your Spirit. Your Body is obvious. It's your flesh and blood. It is the three-dimensional part of you that allows you to see, hear, smell, feel, and taste. Your Mind is your conscious and unconscious mind. This is the part of you that thinks. It takes emotional signals and other electrical signals that the body senses and either stores away in the unconscious or creates a thought based on previously learned factors throughout your life. Those thoughts create your intent and your focus throughout your life, and through this process, you grow in consciousness. Your Spirit, on the other hand, is the part that is often overlooked. It is known by many different names, such as your soul, your Higher Self, your matrix, your aura, or your energy field. It is the part we cannot see, but the part we can feel.

For example, consciously think right now, "I am human." Did you feel the thought happen in your brain? Now be still; perhaps you feel an echo? Perhaps you feel a warmth, or perhaps you hear a softer voice. Where did you feel this? Did it happen in your heart? Most people feel the clear distinction of a conscious thought against a feeling. When you heart breaks, you don't feel it in your head. Your feel it in your heart. This is how your essence talks to you. This is your Higher Self.

Albert Einstein once said: "Concerning matter, we have been all wrong. What we have called matter is energy, whose vibration has been so lowered as to be perceptible to the senses. There is no matter."

Every part of our body has a measurable energy output. In basic terms, even though we cannot see the radio waves, we still know that the radio will work when we switch it on. Your body is a constant flow of energy, and every part of your Whole Self can have an impact on the other. The pain you are feeling emotionally right now, if left to linger and limit you for too long, can and usually does have an impact on your physical body. We all know that stress and anxiety can lead to illness. Even the doctor tells you that. But what a lot of people don't realize is that this pain also has an effect on your spirit. For example, that sore back that you have when you are tense, or when you remember a traumatic event in your childhood, is how a blockage in your spirit is affecting you physically right now.

If you don't like the pain you are dwelling on, the absolute best way to change the way you feel is to change the way you think and act. This is what is known as inner growth.

There is an unspoken *cycle of inner growth* that I have learned and developed over the last few years, and it encompasses seven inner steps in every circumstance. These steps allow you to grow.

These are the seven steps to the cycle of inner growth:

Step 1: **to fall**
Step 2: **to realize the truth**
Step 3: **to reflect within**
Step 4: **to forgive**
Step 5: **to embrace**
Step 6: **to love yourself**
Step 7: **to experience joy**

When you learn to truly love yourself, the pain will no longer affect you as much. That love will give you a sanctuary and provide your life with meaning and hope. As we develop more into the higher vibrations, we discover that it is more important to *be* the right person than to *find* the right person. This means that you need to find contentment within yourself, rather than look for contentment in an outside source. That is the truth I speak of so often. The truth is that only you can control your own happiness.

But how do you do that? ✿

When you fight with love,
You always win because it makes
your opponent look within.

— LIZ BARALLON —

Chapter 3
THE POWER OF BLAME AND FORGIVENESS

"Most of us," said the cosmic humorist, "go through life not knowing what we want, but feeling damned sure this isn't it."
— Ken Keyes

Sometimes when things in life aren't going the way we want them to, we immediately jump into blaming external factors, such as our job, partner, family, lack of money, and so on. However, before we immediately call it quits or run away, it is important to take the time to carefully consider what in your life needs changing to bring about the goal you desire.

If you are constantly saying things like "I feel stuck," "This isn't what I want," "What can I do to change?," "I've got to make a change, but I don't know if I can," then you need to take a step back and really analyze what you are thinking and why you are thinking it, because if you want to change, then it is time to stop any negative beliefs that you can't change.

Whether you believe you can or you can't, you're correct.
— Mark Twain

You need to stop *blaming* for the way your life is, and do something about it. Blame is an uncomfortable word. It is defined as "to feel or declare that [someone or something] is responsible for a fault or wrong." Blame just allows something else to become the scapegoat for your own emotions. A lot of people might be happy just to let life control them and allow blame to become a way to release their own responsibility for their own happiness; however, it would be far more productive to instead take the positive action of deciding to control your own reaction to the circumstances and look at what you need to do to reach your desired outcome.

Negative thinking and worry will only have you going around in circles. I can show you all the best things to do to help get you started on more positive thinking, but the only thing that will help you change is your action. So the choice is yours. What is the worst thing that could happen if you choose to take a step in the direction of change?

When you take responsibility for your own happiness, you not only change your vibration, but you change your outer reality, and you then influence the people around you for the better. Deciding to be happy helps those you love to be happy as well. When you are living to please others, it is easy to trip up, to get confused or stuck. This is because you are living in your perceived notion of what will make someone else happy, which isn't always the reality. This is why it is important to give yourself permission to satisfy yourself first, because then you are giving yourself the gift of self-worth. You give yourself permission to love yourself and then love others. So stop worrying about what others will think of you, and start thinking about what you will think of you if you don't do what lights you up and makes you happy.

To move on from blame, we must learn the art of forgiveness. In my experience I have found that most people have stalled in their growth because of their inability to forgive someone, something, or themselves. Forgiveness is a very hard emotion to achieve. It can be a terribly long journey to forgiveness, and you certainly have no time limit, but once you can achieve forgiveness, you are on your way to the vibration of true happiness. Forgiveness is like the last key on the chain, which you use for the last door in the maze to find the prize. It unlocks and releases pain, and then it allows the wisdom to flow in.

Maybe you are like the old me and say, "I'm happy, and I haven't forgiven such and such," or "I'm happy in not forgiving that person, because they don't deserve my forgiveness." However, if I have learned anything, it is that happiness in your right to be superior isn't the same as true happiness. Until you have learned to forgive, darkness will still surround you, and the only person you are hurting is yourself. And allow me to let you in on a little secret. If you have trouble forgiving someone else, chances are that you haven't yet learned how to forgive yourself.

Psychologists generally define forgiveness as a "conscious, deliberate decision to release feelings of resentment or vengeance toward a person or group who has harmed you, regardless of whether they actually deserve your forgiveness."

Forgiveness isn't about forgetting what someone has done. It isn't about glossing over, excusing, or condoning the actions of the person who has wronged you. You don't have to try to forgive and stay friends or partners with the person, and you don't have to forgive and let go. You can walk away and then forgive, or you can stay and learn to forgive together. That choice is yours alone.

Forgiveness isn't about the other person at all. You may or may not have noticed that not being able to forgive is eating you up inside. You spend far too much of your precious time rehashing the situation and thinking how you would have done things differently, or what you could have said to put the other person in their place. You think of the ways *Karma* could get to them, and you dream about them somehow feeling the same pain they inflicted on you. But what is it doing to you? It's stopping you from living your life to your full potential, and it's stopping you from moving on.

Forgiveness is about you. Forgiveness is allowing you to have peace of mind with no more anger. It involves letting go of deeply hurtful feelings and empowers you to recognize the pain without letting that pain define you. Even more than that, it allows you to have empathy with your offender. It allows you to see that their actions are generally out of pain or misunderstanding. It allows you to see they are probably suffering as well and quite possibly in silence. It doesn't condone what they have done; it has just made it make more sense.

Putting yourself in their shoes and choosing to fight back with love will always win, because it makes the offender look within. Maybe from there they can grow as well. ❁

Forgiveness can be a tough
emotion to crack,
But when you do,
Light and Love seep in
to fill your core.

— LIZ BARALLON —

Chapter 4
THE POWER OF VIBRATIONAL ENERGY

Vibrational Energy is all around us. It is color, sound, music, and light. It is the force that underpins the physical structures of all natural bodies. Subtle energy is the invisible, vital energies that shape physical things. Every cell in your body creates its own measurable vibrating energy. To think like this, we must suddenly see that our whole bodies are a mass of differing vibrational energies coming together harmonically to create our physical being. Our whole being is a wonderful composition of divine music. If the physical being is out of balance, this is an indication of a higher energetic imbalance. Therefore, rather that treating the physical effect alone, the vibrational-energy theory asks that we look at the higher invisible cause.

We can see proof of this vibrational energy in many ways, including a ripple in water, or watching magnetic iron filings move in response to a magnetic current, or the way the Fibonacci spiral, which is also known as the golden ratio or God's thumbprint, manifests itself in most organisms. We can see the Fibonacci spiral in things like your fingerprints, flowers, shells, and even the universe. This energy is a part of all of us.

In fact, we are all energy vibrating on different frequencies broadcasting our own individuality. But we are still all part of the same energy source. This is what I call our Creator Source, Our Love Source, or God Consciousness. It brings new meaning to "I am one with The Force; The Force is with me," the mantra that Chirrut chants in *Rogue One: A Star Wars Story* (for all you *Star Wars* fans—or maybe that's just me).

Nonphysical energy can be accessed and transformed through many methods without requiring any physical contact. This energy can flow, transform, remain stagnant, or even transfer and affect what it comes into contact with. Even your thoughts and emotions have measurable energy.

Let's put that into a practical sense. If you can imagine being stuck in your negative emotions, think about exactly what that is doing to you for a moment. Say, for instance, that you cannot forgive something/someone in your life. You are filled with rage, but you still have to function and look after your family. However, your thoughts are far from loving. Imagine what will happen when your little child comes up to you crying, telling you that they have been hurt. Do you bend over and cuddle them and let them cry into your chest, or do you snap at them, telling them, "Don't be a baby" or "Pull your head in. You will be fine!" Your emotions right now are putting out the energy relating to that

Evidence of the Fibonacci spiral in nature, showing a shell.
© Liz Barallon

Evidence of the Fibonacci spiral in nature, showing a sunflower.
© Magicillustrator | Dreamstime.com

Evidence of the Fibonacci spiral in nature, showing a daisy.
© Waza81Shotz by permission

emotion. It is dictating everything you do. You are allowing that emotion to control you.

Another example would be if you were to walk into a room filled with people who are all having fun. They are excited and enjoying their time. The minute you walk into the room, you would feel that happy energy, and you might even say, "Wow, this energy is great. I'm having a great night!" Then let's imagine that a few people started bickering, and those emotions formed into a fight that went on to involve a few more people. You might then feel the energy of that room change into a fearful, angry, and hateful place.

So even though we think our thoughts are our own, in actual fact, other people are feeling them through the energy that those thoughts put out. Just as you feel the energy of other people around you, they are feeling your negative energy. They are feeling your sadness, anxiety, and despair.

On the other hand, imagine that you are stuck in your happy feelings. Imagine that today you feel so happy and kind and that everything you look at is beautiful and amazing. You see a homeless man on your walk, and instead of thinking, "Oh my goodness, he smells bad; I need to move along quickly," you see his beautiful lost soul, also on its own journey of ascension, and you ask him how he is. Now let's imagine how that small change in attitude could change both of your lives. You continue on with your happy day, knowing that your smile has made a difference to that man. He feels amazing because someone took the time to acknowledge that he even existed.

How powerful are we that our thoughts and emotions have energy that is capable of changing other people's thoughts and emotions? How powerful are we that our thoughts and emotions can affect a large crowd? How powerful are we? Christie Sheldon, in her course Love and Above, claims that by simply raising your vibration to be one in tune with *love*, you can counterbalance the lower energetic vibrations of about 750,000 other people. Imagine if just thirty people tried to raise their vibration of thoughts and emotions. Imagine being able to counterbalance and possible affect 22,500,000 people with the love and happiness vibration. How nice would the world be then?

Loving thoughts can change everything. Choosing the Energy of Forgiveness, Love, and Kindness can not only change your life, it can change the world—one person at a time. So how do you get there?

In the same way that your body can heal physically, you can also heal emotionally. In fact, healing emotionally can help lead to physical healing. You hold the power to change negative emotions, which affect your relationships and all aspects of your life, into loving and positive emotions.

All emotions are electrical impulses and *signals* to your body to act. The body experiences different emotions in different ways. For example, fear increases adrenaline, allowing you to run or fight if you need to. In contrast, happiness causes an *increased activity* in the brain center that actually *inhibits negative* feelings and causes an increase in available energy. *It also limits the ability to even have negative thoughts.* How powerful is that! By just allowing yourself to be happy, you will in turn decrease your ability to give a negative thought any energy at all. Being happy makes you skim completely over the negative, right to the positive. That's how powerful your thoughts are!

With a bit of attention and practice, it is possible to tune your mind to stay optimistic and determined. You can't control the negative emotions and when they arise, but you can control the duration of them and eventually how they arise. If you allow these emotions to stay longer than they should, then you are inviting depression, anxiety, and stress, and it can leave you feeling physically ill and emotionally drained. This prolonged mental state can even completely stop your body's ability to heal itself. That's how powerful your thoughts are!

Your mind is made up of two parts: your conscious mind and your unconscious mind. The emotions and feelings that you are actually aware of are part of your conscious mind, but generally they are repercussions of ingrained unconscious mind thoughts. These are emotions from the past buried deep within the unconscious that we don't even necessarily remember. For example, this ingrained emotion and way of thinking may have been caused by a comment made by a parent when you were only a young child that your artwork was a bit messy and needed a little bit more color. As a child you may have interpreted this as your parent actually saying, "I hate your artwork, and you are not talented at art whatsoever." That then became your belief while growing up, and you might have never tried again to do any art because of it.

These types of unconscious memories, however, might be from more-painful experiences, and because of that, you are suffering now. Often it is these unconscious emotions and thoughts that leave you feeling overwhelmed with anger, guilt, anxiety, sorrow, jealousy, or frustration, without any idea about how to explain why you are feeling this way. Sometimes you don't need to remember the reason you are feeling this way. You simply need to acknowledge the emotion you are having, and create the intention to turn it around. This act alone can give you the power to move on and overcome the pain. It is when you stifle the emotion and let it dwell in your unconscious that it causes energy blocks. Continuing to suppress these feelings is affecting you as a whole on an energetic and physical level, and it is important that you find a healthy way to release the emotion, learning forgiveness so that you can move on. ✿

Sometimes you don't need to remember the reason you are feeling this way.
You simply need to acknowledge the emotion you are having and create the intention to turn it around.

— LIZ BARALLON —

Chapter 5

THE POWER OF
INTENTIONAL THOUGHT

Your spiritual journey is like climbing a mountain. Imagine that our Source is at the top of that mountain, shining down the constant source of energy that we all pull from. Imagine it like the harmony of musical notes from which we create our individual song. Now imagine humanity all climbing the mountain, bathed in that energy that gives us the ability to move. Some people are down at the bottom still, just looking up, simply overwhelmed with the height they need to climb. Some people have made it a little way up, and they are looking back down, wondering if they are doing the right thing without knowing where they will actually end up. Others have made it halfway up with their eyes focused sideways, losing focus on the goal and wondering what other people are doing. Then there are some close to the top, with their eyes directly on the Source at the top, focused on reaching their destination and their ultimate goal.

This scenario represents the differences in all of us on our life journey. Some people feel happy on the ground, not thinking about it, but just looking up and knowing there is something else. Others are determined to find out a little more, but they are unsure of what they have been taught and are questioning what they believe in. Maybe they are halfway up in their journey and have looked sideways to see what everyone else is doing, and believing and possibly looking for someone else's belief to blindly follow. Or perhaps they have found their own truth and live their lives with their heart firmly focused and with the ability to manifest their goals and desires to create the reality that they truly want.

Each and every one of us believes in a different reason for life. Spirituality is not associated with any religion and can be incorporated into all of them. Spirituality is getting in touch with your spiritual side or your Higher Self and learning to understand who you are, holistically. Our beliefs will always resonate with our own gut instinct, soul, or Higher Self. Spirituality is about your individual journey to find your truth within. To find out what makes you happy.

To understand how you can change your intentional thought process around, it is important to understand that you must take a journey into your own spirituality. Your spirituality is your own personal journey, but I will guide you into the fundamentals of the power of intentional thinking and the vibrational frequency it can create.

Cymatics is a great visual example of how a vibrational frequency can have an effect on matter. The German musician and physicist Ernst Chladni noticed in the eighteenth century that when he used a violin bow on a metal plate, it would displace the fine layer of sand covering the plate to form a shape. Each frequency would produce a different geometrical shape.

Perhaps the most popular theory of recent history would be that of Dr. Masaru Emoto, who believed that water was a "blueprint for our reality" and that emotional vibrational energies could change the physical structure of water. Dr. Emoto's famous water crystal experiment consisted of exposing water in glasses to different words, pictures, or music. Water crystals emerge for only twenty to thirty seconds, as the temperature rises and the ice starts to melt, giving us a rare glimpse into the magical world of water crystals and its particular energy with microscopic photography. Dr. Emoto found that water exposed to positive words and thoughts would result in "beautiful crystals" being formed when that water was frozen, and that negative words would produce "ugly," frozen crystal formations.

You disgust me   You fool   Imagination/Hope

Truth   Rising in Love / Harmony   Love/Gratitude

The images of the water crystals produced when subjected to the labeled emotions and thoughts. Reproduced with permission from the Hado Institute © Office, Masaru Emoto, LLC

Although Dr. Emoto described his experiments as a new form of art rather than science or religion, his water crystal experiments hit a nerve among the mainstream scientific community and are considered highly controversial.

This is the problem with any scientific research of theoretical physics that crosses over and merges with the public perception of what is "mysticism." The line is blurred. The condemnation that any research like this will face is huge, simply because there are many out there who stand to lose a lot if "mysticism" is proven to be correct in any way.

Dr. Emoto's experiments became a lifeline to many spiritualists. The world of spiritualism saw this as proof that the vibrational frequency of emotions and thoughts can affect other substances. His experiments have been duplicated many times by countless believers all over the world. You can try it yourself with a few jars of rice, sealed for thirty days. Write your love or hate message on each jar, show the intentional thought of that emotion to the rice each day for thirty days, and then note the difference.

I have a personal belief that the outcome has to do with your intention. If you *intentionally* go into the experiment to prove it wrong, then it will not work, because your intention caused the result. However, if you *intentionally* start the experiment to prove it right and because you believe in the result, then the experiment will work for you. After all, the experiment is about capturing the energy of intentional thought and true emotions. Not fake ones.

Intentional thoughts are those thoughts you actively choose to pursue throughout your day. Reactive thoughts are those thoughts that try to make sense of external circumstances and sensory input. *Together, your intentional thoughts, your reactive thoughts, and your emotions, go toward creating your reality within your consciousness.* Observing the above experiment on the effect of intentional thoughts and emotion on a water crystal, and knowing that the human body is 70 percent water, it wouldn't be a huge leap of faith to conclude that you would be able to guide your own physical vibration and energy with your intentional thoughts!

Together, your intentional thoughts, your reactive thoughts, and your emotions, go toward creating your reality within your consciousness.

— LIZ BARALLON —

Chapter 6
THE POWER OF CONSCIOUSNESS

George Vithoulkas and Dafin F. Muresanu took the time to establish the difference between consciousness and conscience in a study called "Conscience and Consciousness: A Definition," published in the *Journal of Medicine and Life* in 2014. While your conscience is, in basic terms, the determiner of right, wrong, fair, and just, it is much harder to discuss the intricacies of the consciousness. They stated that consciousness is the process of the human mind that receives information from the five senses, which is processed by imagination and emotions, allowing for reason to judge the information to determine whether it should be stored in the memory or discarded.

Vithoulka and Muresanu split consciousness into the two main components of awareness and wakefulness—awareness being the content of your consciousness, and arousal being the level of your consciousness. This awareness encompasses self-awareness in your thoughts, emotions, reflection, and imagination, and also your perception of your external environment through your five senses and electrical signals.

There are many theories of what consciousness actually is, and it is important to note that no one truly knows yet exactly what constitutes consciousness.

Quantum physics theorizes consciousness to be the art of self-observation. This theory states that consciousness creates itself through unconscious processes that are created simply by self-awareness, implying a continually changing brain structure through self-learning. From this view, practicing the art of focusing attention produces measurable changes in spontaneous brain activity by increasing gamma frequencies, which are electromagnetic frequencies. These electromagnetic changes produce physical changes to the brain, both in the dynamic white-matter changes like increased myelination and connectivity, and increased cortical thickness. In other words, these studies prove that focused thoughts produce electromagnetic frequencies that have a direct physical affect on the brain.

The electromagnetic-field theories of consciousness propose that consciousness results when a brain produces an electromagnetic field with specific characteristics. This electromagnetic energy vibrates or pulses, and with every pulse, your electromagnetic energy both broadcasts and attracts. Your energy field transmits your vibrations and magnetizes other similar vibrations into your energy field. You are constantly broadcasting your own energy and attracting external energy or electrical signals.

The unified field theory of consciousness assumes that consciousness is a single unified entity. This theory states that there are three types of consciousness with three hierarchical levels: microconsciousness, macroconsciousness, and the unified consciousness. There is research in the arena of unified field theory that says, and allegedly proves, that *the* unifying force is *Consciousness*. Do we all share the one consciousness?

It is important to know that the unified field theory was a term originally coined by Einstein, after his theory of relativity failed to align with quantum theory. It is also known as the "theory of everything" because it joins two or more of the four interactions, which are electromagnetic, gravitational, weak, and strong, that were previously described by separate theories. Finding the theory of everything is considered the "holy grail" to physicists. So you can imagine there is still much debate about the findings of this research.

A study done by John S. Hagelin called "Is Consciousness the Unified Field? A Field Theorist's Perspective" through Maharishi International University and published in the *Journal of Modern Science and Vedic Science* in 1989 supposedly showed that superstring theory's "unified field" was identical to what Maharishi Mahesh Yogi called the "unified field of consciousness." Hagelin proposed that consciousness is an essential component of the natural world, and that practitioners of transcendental meditation can experience a state of consciousness "in which the observer, the process of observation, and the observed are unified." This, he argued, is the experience of the unified field of physics.

The latest approach to consciousness comes from the Dutch scientist Pim van Lommel. As a cardiologist, he was baffled by many near-death experiences of his patients and the clarity of their memories of the events they experienced while "clinically dead." In his book *Consciousness beyond Life: The Science of the Near-Death Experience*, van Lommel states that "The mind seems to contain everything at once in a timeless and placeless interconnectedness. The information is not encoded in any form of medium, but is stored non-locally as wave functions in nonlocal space, which also means that all information is always and everywhere immediately available." In this theory, van Lommel indicates that the brain is a transceiver for information from these wave functions. The brain does not *produce* consciousness, but instead *facilitates* consciousness.

If we were to assume that an element of truth is in all the theories of consciousness, as well as Dr. Emoto's water crystal results, you can see how you can *intentionally attune yourself to the vibration you desire to be.* All you need to do is consciously decide to guide your thoughts. *Simply being consciously aware of your consciousness is an amazing advancement!* And that is only part of the story, but a good starting point. ❁

Becoming consciously aware of your consciousness is the first step to becoming a butterfly.

— LIZ BARALLON —

Chapter 7

THE POWER OF
HABITUAL FREQUENCY

Human nature dictates that you become comfortable in a place you feel safe. This is how you habitually end up in the same situation over and over again. It is also how you end up stuck in the same thought process or worse in your own emotional distress. Your thoughts, behaviors, and emotions will fluctuate, but you will always come back to rest in your habitual state of mind. Regardless of what you are feeling at the moment, this is the main focus of what needs to change. It is your habitual state of mind that dictates the way you see the world, the way you think and feel, and ultimately your reality.

At which frequency do you normally and habitually lie?

Let me take a moment here to give you an example, and yet again I am going to use a movie allegory. Have you seen *Inside Out*? It features characters that represent our main emotions in control at "Head Quarters" inside little Riley's body. There is Joy, Sadness, Fear, Disgust, and Anger. One of the story lines in this movie is Joy's journey to realize that Sadness isn't just an annoying emotion to control or ignore, but that sadness is vitally important in allowing Riley to realize the truth of happiness. One of the other probably less noticeable story lines to note is that Riley, who is a ten-year-old child, has Joy as her main emotion in control. Happiness rules her thinking. But when we look at the mother, Sadness is the main emotion in control, and in the father, Anger is the main emotion in control. Now, as stereotypical as this seems, just think for a moment: Which emotion would be at your main control right now? Would it be Joy, Sadness, Anger, Fear, or Disgust? This is what I mean by habitually happy. You want to aim for Joy to always be your main emotion in control. You can fluctuate through the other emotions, but you always want to come back to happy.

In particular when dealing with children, it is important to remember that they absorb your energy. They absorb this frequency from your emotions and your thoughts, just as you absorbed your parents' emotional frequencies when you were a child. Usually, however, a child will think that your sadness is their fault, and carry that into their own adulthood. For this reason it is truly important to work on your own habitual frequency in order to pass on good emotional habits and good frequencies to your children.

Elevating your emotions is a process directly related to your ability to use your thoughts to control and maintain your emotions to be in the higher levels. When I say control your emotions, I don't mean to overshadow or smother your lower emotions in order to block them out, but I mean to guide them to a better place. To do this you need to take each situation and strive for that higher thought. The higher thought that allows you to look at all sides and find the positive in the situation. To do this, you need to at least know the scales of emotions and where you lie on that scale.

To study emotions and how they fluctuate, we should take a look at the many available studies of emotions. There are a few different scales, all with a great deal of merit.

Abraham-Hicks Emotional Scale—Jerry and Esther Hicks, *Ask and It Is Given: Learning to Manifest Your Desires*, 2004.

Esther Hicks is an American inspirational speaker and author. She has co-written nine books with her husband, Jerry Hicks, and together they created the Abraham-Hicks Publications, which teaches the law of attraction. According to Esther Hicks, the emotional scale was "translated from a group of non-physical entities called Abraham." Hicks describes what she is doing as tapping into "infinite intelligence."

Interestingly, she joins a number of creative inventors who claim that their ideas were "Channeled" or given to them in a "dream" or simply "Inspired."

Her version of the emotional scale in their book *Ask and It Is Given* is a scale of our feelings and emotions, in sequence from our highest vibrational feelings to our lowest.

As Abraham explains, to "raise your vibration" it is easiest to travel through the emotions from one to the next, rather than try to leap all the way to the top. For example, if you were to be feeling pessimistic, it would be easier to achieve a vibration that resonated at boredom than it would be to jump all the way to feeling joyful and empowered. From boredom you could then reach for contentment, then hopefulness, and then continue all the way up one step at a time.

Centers of Consciousness—Kenneth Keyes, *Handbook to Higher Consciousness*, 5th edition, 1993.

Ken Keyes Jr. was an American personal-growth author and lecturer, and the creator of the Living Love method, a self-help system. Keyes wrote fifteen books on personal-growth and social-consciousness issues, and it was in his book *Handbook to Higher Consciousness* that he developed the scale of the "Centers of Consciousness." Essentially, in 1972 he developed twelve pathways to Higher Consciousness and seven Centers of Consciousness that will enable you to measure your pattern of growth toward higher consciousness. This scale consists of three lower Centers of Consciousness (Security, Sensation, and

Power), and four higher Centers of Consciousness (Love, Cornucopia, Conscious-Awareness, and Cosmic Consciousness). He calls this the Living Love System, and it works best if you simply stay with it and notice in a quiet, accepting, meditative way where you are from moment to moment.

I find Keyes's ideas very thought provoking, and I would recommend that you read his book if you haven't already done so. He talks of emotional addictions created through our culture. For example, to be happy we need that new car, or to have a fridge full of food, or a university degree. But these are simply "prestigious" things we desire, which, once we obtain them, can never truly bring us happiness. Once we have the desired object, we lose interest and want the next best thing that comes along. Objects do not create happiness. We are simply trapped in the never-ending cycle of materialism. "If I could just buy that new house!" Now the car to go with the house. Now the new patio so we can have visitors over. Now the dining table to seat those visitors. We are so focused on the what-ifs and the desire that we forget about the real and the enjoyment of life right now. We forget that living moment to moment with those you love is the way to find happiness. And, most importantly, we forget that looking within and finding our own light is the way to find true inner happiness.

Solfeggio Harmonics—Leonard G. Horowitz and Joseph Puleo, *Healing Codes for the Biological Apocalypse*, 1999.

Solfeggio harmonics is not known as an emotional scale in the typical sense and has been taught mainly as a musical scale. However, you resonate and vibrate at different frequencies along with every cell of your body. Every thought and mental state vibrates and has its very own optimum frequency. Therefore, as humans, we are sound. We are walking symphonies of harmonic vibration, and so is everything else in all of creation. The importance of Solfeggio harmonics is that these tones have been found to resonate with particular emotions or life changes. They also create a similar vibration in their frequencies, as shown in water crystals, to those of particular emotions and particular thought energy.

The original theory of Solfeggio harmonics is that it is an ancient six-tone scale sequence of electromagnetic frequencies. These particular frequencies were rediscovered by Dr. Puleo, a naturopathic physician and one of America's leading herbalists. In his search for the "lost" Solfeggio musical scale, he was inspired to examine the Bible, where he uncovered in the book of Numbers, chapter 7, verses 12–83, that there were patterns of six repeating codes around a series of sacred numbers: 3, 6, and 9. When these were deciphered using the ancient Pythagorean method of reducing the verse numbers to single digits, Puleo claimed the codes showed a series of six electromagnetic sound frequencies that correspond to the six missing tones of the ancient Solfeggio scale: Ut, Re, Mi, Fa, Sol, and La. Although only six were found in the Bible, he quickly deduced three more notes that should be added mathematically to this scale: the frequencies 174 Hz, 285 Hz, and 925 Hz, which when added in with the six original Solfeggio frequencies create three perfect triads of notes ($3 \times 3 = 9$). Puleo then determined that 9 is the sacred number of completion and harmony. It is important to note that both Nikola Tesla and Keely Smith said, "If you only knew the power of the 3s, 6s, and 9s!"

In those times, the musical scale was called a "just intonation." The ancient method of just intonation featured pure intervals between every note that were mathematically related by ratios of small whole numbers (as described earlier), leading to a much-purer sound.

These frequencies were lost because of the change from just intonation to the twelve-tone equal temperament that has become the standard scale since the 1500s due to a need for conformity between various instruments. However, the change left the total harmony of the original scale to disappear.

But Puleo suggests that the vibrations were always there. Only the knowledge concerning them was kept hidden for a long time.

Puleo's theory is that the Solfeggio is actually an ancient musical scale, which had been used by monks in their Gregorian chants. It was suspected that the scale had been deliberately buried in the Vatican vaults because of its effectiveness in mystical healing (or connection to "witchcraft"), which undermined the power and control of the Catholic Church. Professor Will Apel wrote, "The origin of what is now called Solfeggio . . . arose from a Medieval hymn to John the Baptist, which has this peculiarity that the first six lines of the music commenced respectively on the first six successive notes of the scale, and, therefore, it meant that the first syllable of each line was sung to a note one degree higher than the first syllable of the line that preceded it."

The names of the notes were taken from the first stanza of the hymn to St. John the Baptist:

Ut queant laxis Resonare fibris
Mira gestorum Famuli tuorum
Solve polluti Labii reatum

Literal translation from Latin:
"In order that the slaves might resonate [resound] the miracles [wonders] of your creations with loosened [expanded] vocal chords. Wash the guilt from [our] polluted lip. Saint John."

Below are the suggested meanings of these frequencies by Puleo and his team.

Ut: 396 Hz – turning grief into joy, liberating guilt, and fear
Re: 417 Hz – undoing situations and facilitating change
Mi: 528 Hz – transformation and miracles, repairing DNA
Fa: 639 Hz – relationship, connecting with spiritual family
Sol: 741 Hz – expression/solutions, cleaning, and solving
La: 852 Hz – returning to spiritual order

In 1998, Dr. Glen Rein of the Quantum Biology Research Lab in New York performed experiments with in vitro DNA. Four styles of music, including Gregorian chants that use the Solfeggio scale, were converted to scalar audio waves and played via a CD player to test tubes containing in vitro DNA. The effects of the music were determined by measuring the DNA test tube samples' absorption of UV light after an hour of exposure to the music.

Incredibly, Gregorian chants had caused a 5–9.1 percent increase in the absorption of UV light due to the unwinding of the DNA helix. Sanskrit chanting caused a similar 5.8–8.2 percent effect. Rock was only 0–1 percent, and classical music was only 0–1.1 percent, meaning they had little or no effect on DNA. Glen Rein finally concluded that the audible sound waves of the Solfeggio scale can cause resonance in DNA and can have profound healing effects.

The frequency of 528 Hz has become particularly popular due to the fact that is called the miracle frequency. This miracle frequency is said to vibrate at the same frequency as the emotion of love, so it is known as the love frequency. Interestingly and excitingly, since the study, it has been rumored that biochemists have been using the 528 Hz frequency to repair and heal DNA. The good news is that since this study, many artists have created songs tuned to the Solfeggio scale, and many beautiful pieces can be played to help your body heal in these particular frequencies.

Something I also find fascinating, and a little sidenote to get you thinking, is the theoretical research suggesting that pyramids were built and used as hospitals or healing chambers. It was found that the acoustics in a pyramid could create the perfect frequencies and harmony for healing, similar to the way we use tuning forks or singing bowls today to heal with sound. The researchers also surmised that the frequencies could be used to take the "patient" into a deep meditative state.

Again, as with any great energetic theory, the Solfeggio harmonics come up against a lot of backlash. According to some skeptics, when the tones are played together, the harmony isn't complete. Although the musical tones of these frequencies could be disputed, I do not refute Puleo's claims of the hidden code in the Bible, because I even went and checked that myself. His Hidden (9) code is completely correct. In studying the book of Numbers myself, I also found some amazing codes. It is my belief that the Solfeggio harmonics are literally the frequencies of certain emotions, or to be more accurate, growth stages in emotional elevation. In my own conclusion, I discovered that the Bible has its very own emotional scale.

Below is my interpretation after reading through this section of the Bible myself.

174 Hz: Acknowledging the truth and how to achieve it. *Truth of union in harmony.*

285 Hz: Releasing judgment. *Bad Decisions hide the truth in the midst of your journey.*

396 Hz: Release of pain and suffering. *Invest in the harmony within.*

417 Hz: Aiming for balance. *Complete Harmony is the truth of completion and union.*

528 Hz: Balance brings healing and success. *In the midst of the journey home, there will be new beginnings.*

639 Hz: Gratefulness for inner growth. *Inner investment leads to balance and harmony.*

As the story emerges through these stages, I can see that the Solfeggio harmonics is a hidden code explaining the instructions of balancing your emotions through going up the emotional scale to give up the "evil" or "hell" of anger, fear, and judgment to return to the "heaven" of the harmony of balance and be complete and grateful for your inner happiness.

The Emotional Scales

When you look at these emotional scales, where do you think you habitually lie on the emotional scale? Do you feel like you are constantly worrying about many things beyond your control? Do you feel like you are always looking on the negative side of the situation? Or are you someone who looks for the hopeful things to focus on? Look at the scales carefully, and as you go through each emotion, take the time to grab that emotion and feel it. Then ask yourself, Is this something I feel a lot? Does this feeling sit with me constantly throughout the day? Now is the time to be completely honest with yourself and give yourself the gift of acknowledgment. Perhaps you fluctuate between two or three emotions, or maybe you are sitting within one emotion at the moment. There is no "normal" here, and this isn't necessarily a permanent thing. It is just *your* stage of *your* journey. However, if you can acknowledge the journey and become conscious of it, you can then guide it with purpose.

The Emotional Scales

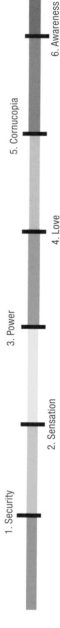

Abraham-Hicks Emotional Scale Key

22. Fear/Grief/Depression/Despair
21. Insecurity/Guilt/Unworthiness
20. Jealousy
19. Hatred/Rage
18. Revenge
17. Anger
16. Discouragement
15. Blame
14. Worry
13. Doubt
12. Disappointment
11. Overwhelment
10. Frustration/Impatience/Irritation
9. Pessimism
8. Boredom
7. Contentment
6. Hopefulness
5. Optimism
4. Belief / Positive Expectation
3. Enthusiasm/Eagerness
2. Passion
1. Appreciation/Freedom/Love

ABRAHAM-HICKS EMOTIONAL SCALE

22 21 20 19 18 17 16 15 14 13 12 11 10 9 8 7 6 5 4 3 2 1

KENNETH KEYES CENTRES OF CONSCIOUSNESS

1. Security
2. Sensation
3. Power
4. Love
5. Cornucopia
6. Awareness
7. Cosmic Consciousness

The Emotional Scale Comparison. Images created © Liz Barallon. Images included with permission from the Hado Institute. © Office, Masaru Emoto, LLC. Information referenced from Ask It Is Given, Learning to Manifest Your Desires; Abraham-Hicks. © by Jerry & Esther Hicks. Handbook to Higher Consciousness, Ken Keyes Jr.; Healing Codes for the Biological Apocalypse, Leonard G Horowitz and Joseph Puleo. Hebrew Interlinear Bible (OT), Numbers, 7:12–83; Scripture4all Foundation.

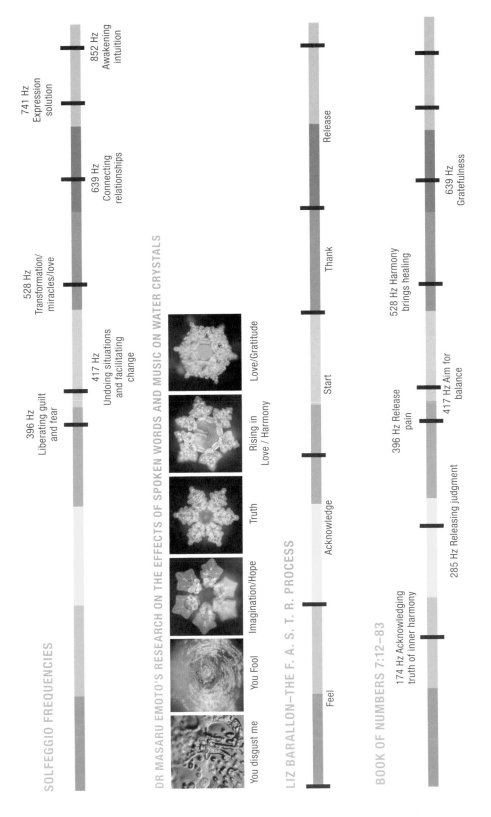

SOLFEGGIO FREQUENCIES

396 Hz Liberating guilt and fear

417 Hz Undoing situations and facilitating change

528 Hz Transformation/ miracles/love

639 Hz Connecting relationships

741 Hz Expression solution

852 Hz Awakening intuition

DR MASARU EMOTO'S RESEARCH ON THE EFFECTS OF SPOKEN WORDS AND MUSIC ON WATER CRYSTALS

You disgust me

You Fool

Imagination/Hope

Truth

Rising in Love / Harmony

Love/Gratitude

LIZ BARALLON–THE F. A. S. T. R. PROCESS

Feel

Acknowledge

Start

Thank

Release

BOOK OF NUMBERS 7:12–83

174 Hz Acknowledging truth of inner harmony

285 Hz Releasing judgment

396 Hz Release pain

417 Hz Aim for balance

528 Hz Harmony brings healing

639 Hz Gratefulness

The F.A.S.T.R. Emotion Process

The emotional scales listed above help us understand our *negative vibration* vs. our *positive vibrations*; however, we have nothing really simple and concrete that would allow us to step through the emotions easily to help us process them in a healthy way.

Through my personal journey and listening to the journey of others, I have developed this five-step process, which, when turned into a habit, can help you overcome any obstacle or negative emotion.

As you recall, I said that it is good to feel the pain, but not to become stuck in the pain. So we need a series of steps to get ourselves to release the negative emotion and go back to being *habitually happy*. When you have worked through this process a few times, it becomes easier and easier, until you can get so good at it that it can take no time at all to release the pain, see the message of the pain, and appreciate the journey to then rest back in the harmony of your habitual happiness. ✺

STEP TWO:

Acknowledge

Chapter 8
THE POWER OF SELF-LOVE

The next step is to acknowledge the pain. This can actually be the hardest step, and it involves a certain degree of self-honesty and self-perception. These are often things that we turn a blind eye to—or that we will find hidden in our unconscious minds. As you work your way up the emotional scales from the lower vibrations, you will experience things such as self-doubt and frustration and worry, but you will also feel the courage to look within and make the decision to change.

When life gets tough, you can very often lose your sense of self-worth. Quite often you also have to contend with other people putting you down, or even just being blunt in a way that allows misinterpretation of the message, creating your own lack of self-worth to make it worse than it really is.

Being unhappy in yourself is very restrictive. When you can't realize your own worth, you will struggle to strive for more. Do you lack confidence? Do you lack self-love? Do you think others' opinions are more important than yours?

You are not a doormat for other people to walk all over. It is not okay to put others' happiness in front of your own. It is time you learn to accept yourself the way you are and realize that you are worthy of love. And you are worthy of love from the most important person in your life. You!

When you can go within, you no longer need to look for something outside yourself to make you feel "complete." Once you can accept your own faults and learn to either love them or change them, you are able to completely hand yourself over to love. You are worthy. You are amazing and you deserve the best that your dreams can aspire to.

Relearning to love yourself is the start to realizing that you are not a person made to accommodate someone else's whims. You were designed perfectly for you. Loving yourself will illuminate you so that your light can shine so bright wherever you go, leading the way to your divine purpose.

You can be a person who will inspire others to be better versions of himself or herself. More importantly, your aim is to figure out a way to enter into the higher energy vibration of love. *Shhh* . . . here's the secret . . . this doesn't mean being able to love someone else again. This means falling in love with you. This is the release of pain you need.

Let me start by asking you to answer the question "What is your deepest desire?" You know what I mean. What is the one thing that you have never told anyone that you would like to do? I will tell you what mine was. I always wanted to be a Reiki healer. It was something I put to the back of my mind because I was afraid of being "judged." I knew all the benefits, and I could see the logic in it as well as the proof, but I knew that the majority of the world couldn't see this "sense" that I saw in it. The Western media told humanity constantly that humans were merely a reflection of their physical symptoms and nothing more, and unfortunately the brainwash worked for the majority of the people. Reiki is still viewed mostly as fantasy and mysticism, but when you actually experience a correct Reiki healing, you cannot deny that something about it just works. Since Reiki works on the theory of intentional thought energy vibration, I'm sure you can appreciate how it does have merit to be a recognized form of treatment for all sorts of ailments. Energy healing has been around for thousands of years in one form or another, and it obviously has stood the test of time. Even some military departments across the world will use Reiki in their counseling to help treat posttraumatic stress disorder after their members' service for their country.

What is it about you that you are afraid that people will judge you for? Who is the first person who comes to mind when you think of that fear of judgment? Now I want you to focus on that person for a little while. Do you really care what they think of you? Is their friendship that important?

The truth is there is only one person you should care about and what those thoughts of you might be—and that is you! And if your friend truly is your friend, then they will love you and they will not care, or judge, when you go ahead and do what you want to do. If they are not your true friends, then you will know soon enough. In the end, it will not matter, because following your deepest desire will light you up, and in doing that, it will attract the right people and circumstances into your life and eliminate the wrong people and influences from your life. Following your deepest desire is a great step into a better life.

Self-acceptance is key to helping you realize your self-worth. You need to look deep within and realize that there is no such thing as the perfect human being, and it is your imperfections that make you amazing!

To realize your self-worth, it is important to follow five crucial steps.

1. Acceptance

Think about someone whom you really admire. I want you to remember the day you met that person, and remember your first impression of them. Was that person warm, caring, funny, calm, sweet, generous?

Now think about yourself. Imagine meeting yourself for the first time. What thoughts pop to your mind? Are you warm, caring, funny, calm, sweet, generous? Something else? Do you have a lovely smile, or inviting eyes? Are you talented at the art of conversation or great at listening? What is it about you that you love the minute you realize who you really are? You will invariably come up with some negative things you don't like about yourself. We all suffer self-criticism, but this is where you need to learn the art of compassion. Pretend you are a friend meeting you for the first time. Would you even notice that thing you constantly criticize yourself for? If you did notice it, would you care? Would the good outweigh the bad? Would someone else love that about you? Try to understand yourself and not condemn yourself.

Your confidence will rise when you can accept and appreciate your own self-image.

2. Be True to You

Let me introduce you to your ego! This is the voice of "reason." It is the voice that tells you that you can't do that. It is the voice that reasons with you and tells you that other people would judge you. It's the voice that reminds you what your mother said that one time when you were four about your naughty behavior. It's the voice that keeps you "safe." It keeps you safe from stepping outside the comfort zone and safe from striving for more. Safe from fear, but also locked *in* fear. Your ego is there to protect you from further vulnerability.

Your ego also cushions you from reality and limits your visibility. It can diminish your capacity for living the way you truly desire to live.

For one second, try to silence the ego. Try to get in touch with your Higher Self. Listen to your soul's calling! Listen to that inner voice. The one deep down that feels like it comes from the heart. That is the true you.

Becoming more authentic means allowing yourself to think your own thoughts and make your own choices. It means you can rise above the need for approval from others. You no longer feel obligated to anyone. Your feelings, thoughts, and choices are now yours alone. You no longer feel the need to agree, simply to be well mannered. You are happy to agree to disagree.

3. Empathy

Accepting who you are is extremely liberating. It allows you to then be a support to others as well. Reaching out to someone else allows you to move out of yourself in a genuine and caring way.

Learning to place yourself in someone else's position can be liberating. It can help you realize that the world doesn't actually revolve around you. This empathy is the way to diminish misinterpretations in communications, since you are able to understand why someone might do or say what they have done or said. Empathy allows you to feel deeply and spontaneously with others. It allows the gift of understanding and the ability to be kind instead of judgmental.

The world where you can "Feel" what others feel is a world where the possibilities of amazing human experiences are greatly enhanced.

4. Believe

"I am not good enough." Is this what you think? Is this belief firmly hardwired into your core? Somehow, something will always go wrong! If you said yes to this, then you need to stop giving yourself excuses. You need to make the commitment to *believe in yourself*. Truly believing in yourself and your motivations is your ticket to success. Your thoughts give your belief the power, so to change your belief you need to change your thoughts. "I *am* good enough!" There is no longer any such word as *not* or *can't*.

5. Belong

A community is seen as a union of people who have something in common. This could be church, family, friendship circle, book club, the car forum, Tarot club, or the indigo children group. It is so important to realize that even if you feel alone right now, you aren't actually *ever* alone. There is always someone who will "get you." There is always someone who will *understand*. There is always *someone*.

When you can appreciate that there are others whom you can feel comfortable with and experience a sense of mutual belonging, then you will learn how to feel more confident in giving and receiving. Feeling *alone* can drive you into the depths of loneliness and alienation. Feeling alone most importantly undermines your confidence and increases your negative feelings or low self-worth, anger, and resentment. ☼

There is always someone who will "get you." There is always someone who will understand. There is always someone.

— LIZ BARALLON —

Chapter 9
THE POWER OF INTUITIVE LIVING

The path to self-love is sometimes a deep and dark journey within yourself. During this journey, you will also learn who you are at the deeper level. This isn't just your belief about yourself or your ingrained thoughts and opinions. This is your gut instinct, your spirit, and your soul. It is your intuition! That voice that comes from nowhere but has some seriously profound messages!

So often in life we go about listening to others, the media, the latest social opinion, learning from an institution, and we forget to think for ourselves. Our ego tells our instinct that "You are wrong, because the newsman or the teacher said so." We ultimately become brainwashed with other people's ideas of "normal." There is no such thing as "normal"! You are individually you and at the same time part of a collective that is Humanity.

Your intuition is your connection to your Higher Self, your soul, your spirit. This is the true you. Your body and your experiences have all been designed to allow you to grow and learn all the lessons your soul needs to learn. I believe that we are born in grace and love and we die in grace and love, and all that occurs in between in this place we call life is "free choice." It is your choice if you choose to keep wallowing in the grief, anger, and rage of "Hell," or you can choose to build a new home of enlightenment with your rock bottom as your foundation.

If our Creator Source is an energy that resonates at the frequency of love, then our Source doesn't operate in any frequency below love. So Source shouldn't be feared because our Creator isn't capable of fear. Source can't be vengeful because our Creator isn't capable of anger. Source can't judge us when we die because our Creator isn't capable of judgment. When we die, despite our choices in life, our Creator will always welcome us with unconditional love and grace. Source is LOVE! Love is a vibration and possibly the frequency of 528 Hz. That makes our Source SOUND, or as John 1:1 says, "In the beginning was the *word*, and the *word* was with *God*, and the *word* was *God*." Many ancient languages interchange the words "speech" and "sound," so let me write it another way to help you understand what I mean. "In the beginning was the *sound*, and the *sound* was with *love*, and the *sound* was *Love*."

An interesting correlation is that the Hebrew word for God is Elohim. *El* means *might, strength, power*. There is no greater strength than love! The Hebrew word *ohim* has an unknown translation into English apparently. I don't know about you, but to me, it sounds awfully similar to a sound uttered during meditation. In fact, the ancient Hindu sages maintain that the entire cosmos is created through the vibrations of the primordial mantra "Om." This is precisely the reason that they recite this mantra to tune into the consciousness of the primordial tone. And it is theorized that the frequency of Om when uttered is of course 528 Hz.

If, as I suggest, our Creator is the sound of love and therefore a frequency of vibration, then it is possible to feel this frequency of Source within us all. If we can start to vibrate at the love frequency, then we will be one with our Creator and one with each other.

As the ancient Hindu scriptures state, Nada Brahma. The world is sound!

Let me take you on a journey into our past. In 1971, a man named John Lennon sat down at his piano to write a beautiful song that would make number one in the UK after his death and eventually become one of the most played musical pieces for years to come. Why was this piece of music so popular when it held beliefs similar to communism? It was so popular because John was so ahead of his time. His song wasn't about creating a world of common ownership; it was more an idea of everyone living together as one. Avoiding the barriers that divide us, living for the moment, and living in peace. The other reason why his song was so popular is that it was played mostly in the tune of 528 Hz. It was played in the love frequency. The healing song would appeal to the masses, simply because it resonated with them on a deeper level.

Below is a picture of a water crystal encoded with the song "Imagine" by John Lennon.

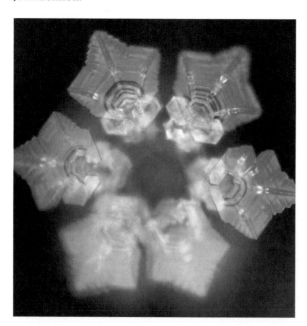

The image of the water crystal produced when playing the song "Imagine" by John Lennon. The Hado Institute © Office Masaru Emoto, LLC

One morning I woke up to a revelation. I had a dream of the beginning of the universe that made so much sense to me that I would like to share it with you all. We hear the saying "As Above, So Below" so often that I think we can sometimes underestimate its importance. Everything in this universe seems to occur in the same pattern and in the same cycles. Let's look, for instance, at your very own creation. As a human, when your parents created you, you were created with love. You were two mere cells coming together to multiply into a human being, and it was that *intentional* love that created you. In my dream I saw that the universe was created with this very same intentional love. One atom coming together with another atom, and together realizing the sound and frequency of intentional love. "Om." The frequency caused by this bonding of atoms caused a multiplication of itself in the form of the pattern of the golden ratio. The golden ratio is also known as the Fibonacci spiral, and it was this frequency and subsequent vibrational pattern that created the stars and planets—and everything else in between. That intentional love energy of our Source runs through everything. It is shown in the flowers, the animals, the vegetables, and even humans. Even as a fetus, we curl into the Fibonacci spiral, and one could argue that the starting point might be our pineal gland. It is known as the seed of the body and is thought to be the part that gives life to your body.

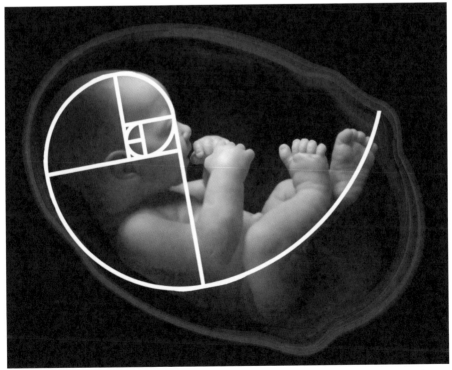

A baby in the womb curled into the Fibonacci spiral, with the starting point in the area of the pineal gland.
© Gonzalomedin | Dreamstime.com

The pineal gland is spiritually thought to be vital in interpreting our intuitive senses, probably because it is so vital in processing the emotional energetic signals. Physically, it hangs from the roof of the completely dark cave of the third ventricle of the brain and is surrounded by cerebral spinal fluid (CSF). The pineal gland was called the "Seat of the Soul" by French philosopher René Descartes and author Alice Bailey. It is thought that the pineal gland is the connection to our soul. It is the caterpillar in its cocoon waiting to emerge as the beautiful butterfly.

The pineal gland is part of the endocrine system and is connected to the thalamus, hypothalamus, basil nuclei, and medial temporal lobe. It is a still a somewhat mysterious gland in that scientists believe there is still more to learn about its function, and most of what they do know is still only theory, and they aren't completely sure of its functions.

What we do know is that the pineal gland is important in regulating emotions. It secretes two neurotransmitter chemicals, melatonin and serotonin. A neurotransmitter chemical essentially acts as a messenger, transmitting the emotional energetic signals across chemical synapses, such as the neuromuscular junction, from one nerve cell to another targeted nerve cell, muscle cell, or gland cell.

Serotonin is a very important chemical because it affects nearly all the brain cells, including those relating to mood, sexual function, appetite, sleep, memory, learning, and temperature regulation. This means that we need our serotonin levels to be balanced in order to process our emotions properly. It is commonly thought that a serotonin deficiency is the cause of depression, and most antidepressants will work on increasing the levels of serotonin in order to help the regulation of the energetic signals of the emotions.

The other place that we find serotonin being produced is in our digestive tract and blood platelets. Researchers know that there are both neural and mucosal sources of serotonin in the digestive tract, but the reason for serotonin being found in the gut is somewhat unclear. Research by Judith J. Wurtman, PhD, and Nina T. Frusztajer, MD, in their book *The Serotonin Power Diet: Eat Carbs—Nature's Own Appetite Suppressant—to Stop Emotional Overeating and Halt Antidepressant-Associated Weight Gain*, shows that serotonin works as an appetite suppressant, telling your brain that you feel full even if you are not. The authors state that there is a carbohydrate-serotonin relationship and that your body can only produce that serotonin when you eat sweet or starchy carbohydrates. They discovered through clinical trials that most people develop a carbohydrate craving at about 3 p.m. every day, and that eating a small portion of sweet or starchy carbohydrate will not only make you feel full but will also make you feel happier and more content, with increased emotional energy. They found that people who naturally followed this craving were "self-medicating" for stress and anxiety.

Not only do we find that serotonin in the gut can help make you feel full and content, but what if that serotonin in the gut also helps with eliminating the lower emotional energetic signals from the body in a *release* method once you have successfully processed them?

The melatonin produced by the pineal gland, in conjunction with the hypothalamus, helps control our circadian rhythms, which are the sleep-wake cycles, our breathing cycles, our awareness of the time of day, and the seasons via the degree of light coming through the retina of the eyes. Another interesting correlation is that the pineal gland actually contains cells just like those in the retina of our eyes. This is also one of the reasons that it is known as the third eye.

Intuitively, the pineal gland is associated with both the Crown and Third-Eye Chakras and acts like an antenna or satellite dish receiving electromagnetic energies through the Crown Chakra. It is associated with intuition or clairvoyance, which is the ability to "see" beyond the physical sense of sight.

When the pineal gland is healthy, we have the potential to learn more from our Higher Self. It is also a healthy and developed pineal gland that allows some people the gift to see, hear, and feel guides, angels, or those who have passed over. It is said that the pineal gland is what connects us with the unknowable, the great mystery, and the great beyond.

Physically balancing the pineal gland can relieve insomnia, jet lag, SAD (seasonal affective disorder), breathing irregularities, and depression. Some believe that dysfunction in the secretion of melatonin may play a part in autism and cancer. Stress, aging, lack of complete darkness when sleeping, not getting enough sleep, electric blankets, and other electromagnetic influences such as TVs and computers have been shown to decrease melatonin secretion. Also, too much melatonin decreases serotonin, and too little melatonin creates too much, which can create agitated states and even psychosis.

Unfortunately, the pineal gland hardens, atrophies, and shrinks as we age, and fluoride, which is a known neurotoxin and known to be detrimental to the pineal gland, is commonly added to our water supply and toothpaste.

To keep your pineal gland healthy and balanced, you could try activities such as meditation, a regular good night's sleep, quiet environments, listening to healing music in tune with the Solfeggio frequencies, exercising, being in nature, reducing chemicals and toxins from your diet, eating a small portion of sweet or starchy carbohydrates daily, drinking fluoride-free filtered water, and buying a fluoride-free toothpaste.

Not only will you find the pineal gland essential in intuition and spirituality, but there is developing evidence that there are other physical parts of our body that receive and transmit energetic vibrations to help interpret and facilitate your intuition.

Your heart is also said to be physically a big player in interpreting your intuition.

I would love to introduce you to another concept of intuitive living in regard to your heart. As we have discussed, 528 Hz "C" is the third note on the Solfeggio harmonic scale, and it relates to the note "Mi" on the scale and derives from the phrase "Mi-ragestorum" in Latin, meaning "miracle." Also, 528 nanometers (nm) relates to the color green (chlorophyll), which, in turn, is related to the Heart Chakra.

Common discussion and standardized education tells us that the brain does the thinking for us. However, there are now theories and trials that show that it is in fact our heart that first detects an external energetic stimulus, which will then relay the message quickly to the brain. A study done by Rollin McCraty, PhD; Mike Atkinson; and Raymond Trevor Bradley, PhD, in 2004 looked at twenty-six participants and showed them thirty calm and fifteen emotionally arousing pictures. The trial measured the skin conductance, the electroencephalogram (EEG), and the electrocardiogram (ECG) to determine the brain and heart response as well as heartbeat decelerations or accelerations in response to the external stimuli. These measurements were used to investigate where and when in the brain and body intuitive information is processed.

Surprisingly, the main findings in relation to the heart's role in intuitive perception were found to be vital, since the heart is the organ that receives and responds to intuitive information *before* the brain. It seems that the heart is involved in the processing and decoding of intuitive information, then sending it on to the brain in the same way as conventional sensory input.

Added to this, they found that there was a significantly greater heart rate deceleration just prior to future emotional stimuli compared to calm stimuli. This indicates that perhaps our heart knows what is coming ahead of time. Are we all clairvoyant?

David Paterson, PhD, a professor at Oxford University, found that your heart also contains thousands of specialized neurons that are located mainly around the right-ventricle surface of the heart, forming a complex network of neurons. Paterson claims that it is this network that allows the brain and heart to communicate.

In addition to functioning as a sophisticated information-processing and information-encoding center, the heart is also an endocrine gland and, therefore, its own chakra, which produces and secretes hormones and neurotransmitters. Thus, with each beat, the heart not only pumps blood but also continually transmits complicated patterns of neurological, hormonal, pressure, and electromagnetic information to the brain and throughout the body.

Physically, the heart, through its extensive interactions with the brain and body, emerges as a critical component of the emotional and intuitive system.

Intuitively, even science is proving that your heart is extremely important, and trusting your Higher Self is vital to acknowledging your feelings and your pain.

When we say "trust your gut instinct," maybe we are actually referring to the stimulus you are feeling in your heart and the emotional release that occurs in your gut.

Your intuition speaks to you all day long and can even produce physical symptoms. Intuition is also known as claircognizance. It is the pure sense of "knowing." For example, you may just have a sense of "knowing" that your job interview tomorrow will go well. It feels separate from words, images, or emotions. It is already there at the back of your mind, waiting for you to acknowledge and listen to it. Intuition can show up as a voice in your head or a vision in your mind's eye (clairvoyance). It can show up in physiological signs in your body, such as goosebumps, or a muscle twitching, a tightness, or even a creepy feeling (clairsentience). It can leave you short of breath or feeling a sense of calm suddenly. If you pay attention to your body and your six senses more, you will be able to listen more to your Higher Self.

If these are things you have trouble tuning in to or feeling, then you may be stopping them through an unconscious fear. Common energetic blockages to being able to listen to your intuition may be fear of the unknown, a closed or blocked Crown Chakra, an overactive mind, lack of practice in listening to your intuition, or even a strong belief that you don't even have an intuition. Simply keep asking your Higher Self to show you these intuitive gifts, and they will come over time. Finding your own intuition or Higher Self is a journey, and without that journey you will miss amazing things. It will require practice and patience and the ability to open up your mind and your belief system. The ability to connect to the world of energy is essential to evolve to a much-higher emotional vibration.

We are purely physical vessels that have the main aim to feel, interpret, process, and produce electromagnetic vibrational energy, and it is you who holds the power to choose which vibration you want to produce.

Learning to listen to your intuition and guide your emotions through a strategic plan, such as my F.A.S.T.R. Process, allows you to habitually rise the lower vibrational emotions to that of love and happiness. I literally mean, let's raise your vibrations to 528 Hz and above. ✾

In the beginning was the sound,
and the sound was with love,
and the sound was Love.

— LIZ BARALLON —

Chapter 10

THE POWER OF EMOTIONS
ON YOUR DNA

Often, when humanity looks for answers, they look to the universe and all things big and unexplained. However, maybe our answers are in the smallest particles in the universe. Perhaps our clues come from thinking small.

Deoxyribonucleic acid, or as it is commonly known, DNA, is the hereditary material in humans and almost all other organisms. Nearly every cell in a person's body has the same DNA. Most DNA is located in the cell nucleus and can make exact copies of itself. Each strand of DNA in the double helix can serve as a pattern for duplicating the sequence of bases. This is critical when cells divide because each new cell needs to have an exact copy of the DNA present in the old cell.

The vital thing needed for DNA to function is phosphorus. In fact, we could not survive without phosphorus. Every cell is surrounded by it in the cell membrane; it is the storage and retrieval part of the DNA and is a vital part of our energy system, being a central molecule in all living cells represented as adenosine triphosphate (ATP).

What is the importance of phosphorus? It is the carrier of your inner light. Literally. Some even say it is the antenna for energy within our DNA and within our body.

The word "phosphorus" came from the ancient Greek word for *light bearer*, and similarly the Latin name for light bearer is *Lucifer*. Contrary to popular religious belief, Lucifer is not actually the devil. It instead refers to the morning star, being the first to bring the light. It could have received its correlation with Satan by being the first to arrive after the darkness of hell. When you are faced with a darkness in pain, the truth of light and love comes forth, and then you begin your journey up the emotional scale again. Lucifer is the light to guide the way.

Only 10 percent of DNA is used for building proteins, and for many years the remaining 90 percent of the DNA molecule was considered "junk DNA"; however, research by Grażyna Fosar and Franz Bludorf, published in their book Vernetzte Intelligenz, indicates that this remainder of the molecule might be basically a means of data storage and communication. Incredibly, what they found was that DNA had a code that followed the same rules as language, as it followed the rules of phrases, semantics, and grammar.

This is why emotions, thoughts, and words have such an effect on our physical bodies. It quite literally is being received by our DNA, which in turn is reacting and transmitting into our physical being.

Now imagine that you carry around with you energy from your thoughts, words, and emotions that the human eye cannot see. When you think of electricity, you know you can't see it in physical form, but you know it's there. It is the same with the body. The body is pure energy, vibrating within our cells, in equilibrium and symbiosis with water, blood, bone, and bacteria to create physical form.

To help you understand, I can't help but make the connection to *Star Wars*. George Lucas describes his fabricated Midi-chlorians as his connection to the "*Force*." They are microscopic, intelligent life forms that originated at the beginning of the universe and were within the cells of all living organisms. They formed a symbiotic relationship with their hosts. The more Midi-chlorians you had, the more sensitive you were to the force. This is how Anakin Skywalker was identified as the possible "chosen one." His Midi-chlorian count was taken through a blood sample, and he was determined to have the most ever found.

All energy from the Living Force, from all things that have ever lived, feeds into the Cosmic Force, binding everything and communicating to us through the Midi-chlorians.

—Qui-Gon Jinn, to Yoda

George Lucas based this theory on our real-life mitochondria. These microscopic organelles live in a symbiotic relationship with every cell in our body. Mitochondria carry a small amount of independent DNA containing thirty-seven chromosomes that help complete the mitochondria's function of producing energy within your cell. They produce oxidized glucose as energy for the cell. It is interesting to correlate that it is thought that billions of years ago, mitochondria were independent bacteria and became part of the eukaryotic cells by a process called endosymbiosis.

Now if you think about the dream I had, which I described earlier in the book, then if you were to imagine this fusion took place with the sound of love energy, then symbiosis might in fact be our original love connection. Symbiosis is love: to take on another living organism and allow each other to coexist for a lifetime to work together as a team to create energy and other amazing processes through dividing and replicating to form life. That's a special sort of bond. It reminds me of love within humans. We want to take on another person to love and to work in a symbiotic relationship to create amazing things, including new life.

So if you can imagine your human coherence as working in symbiosis with others, perhaps you can find a greater connection to humanity—the type you need to evolve into enlightenment.

To further prove the point on this theory, I would love to show you few scientific trials throughout the last century.

The first one I would like to tell you about was a study done by P. P. Gariaev and Vladimir Poponin, "Vacuum DNA Phantom Effect In Vitro and Its Possible Rational Explanation," published in the journal *Nanobiology* in 1995. In this study, they placed light photons (particles of light) in a scattering-chamber vacuum and observed their behaviors. When the photons are by themselves in the vacuum, they have no pattern and seem to just hang in space. However, for some reason, the scientists decided to place a sample of human DNA in the scattering chamber with the light photons, and they found that the photons would follow the DNA's geometrical pattern, even after the DNA sample was taken away, performing in a memory of the coded information. "Surprisingly and counter-intuitively," they were able to observe that DNA does affect our physical world. They went on to say, "We are forced to accept the possibility of some new field of energy."

The second study is one that was undertaken by Glen Rein, PhD, and Rolin McCraty, PhD, published as "Structural Changes of Water and DNA Associated with New Physiologically Measurable States" in the *Journal of Scientific Exploration* in 1994. In this study, the researchers placed human DNA into a double-sealed jar to ensure that there were no outside effects on the reactions within the sealed jar. They then asked five people who were highly trained in the ability to control their emotions through different emotive methods to project certain emotions for five minutes while holding the jar with the DNA and water samples. The most-interesting results were the findings of our lower emotions. When the double-sealed jars were subjected to lower emotions from our emotional scale, the human DNA would tighten to the point where it was no longer functional to its full extent. They also found that when the DNA was exposed to the higher emotions from our emotional scale that the DNA would relax and stretch out, allowing all its information to be utilized to its full extent. The researchers concluded, "Human emotion produces effects that defy conventional laws of physics."

Through these studies they were able to prove something that our ancient ancestors have told us all along: that our emotions affect our DNA, and our DNA affects our physical world. Does this mean, again, that we have proof that our emotions can change our physical world?

This is simple epigenetics, which is the study of how your environment affects gene expression, or how genes are turned on or off. A gene expression is the process where the genetic code in the DNA is instructed to produce structures and molecules within your cells. *Dominating energetic waveforms* in the body potentially have the *strongest* epigenetic influence. That means that your *habitual emotional frequency* potentially has the greatest effect on influencing the instructions that your DNA gives to manifest physical structures within your cells. Ultimately, this habitual emotional frequency has the greatest effect on *your physical body and the changes that occur in your physical body, such as illness over the course of your lifetime.* The question is, What emotions are your dominating energetic waveforms? What is your habitual emotional frequency?

Some might say that our physical world can affect our emotions. This is true, but only if you let it. Controlling your intentional thoughts to elevate your emotions to habitually live in happiness is the goal you need to focus on. ❁

Controlling your intentional thoughts to elevate your emotions to habitually live in happiness is the goal you need to focus on.

— LIZ BARALLON —

Chapter 11

THE POWER OF THE REALIZATION THAT YOU HOLD THE POWER

In 1909, there was a study done that proved that reality only exists when you observe it. A study such as this in the early 1900s sent the scientific community into a buzz, as nobody could quite explain it. It was called the double-slit experiment, and it observed that particles of light, otherwise known as photons, act in waves *only* when being *observed*. If the light wasn't being observed, then it would be random. So it seemed that conscious awareness created a reality to appear.

It actually reminds me of asking a child to do something, then, once leaving the room, finding that the child—thinking that no one is watching them—will play around and act completely randomly, doing what they want. However, when the child realizes they are being watched, they start behaving and doing what they were meant to do. What if photons have a consciousness of their own? What if they only act in waves when they are doing what they have been asked to do?

In 1998, scientists who wanted to take this reality theory a little further undertook another study. Professor Mordehai Heiblum, PhD; Eyal Buks; Ralph Schuster, PhD; Diana Mahalu, PhD; and Vladimir Umansky, PhD, from the Weizmann Institute of Science, published "Quantum Theory Demonstrated: Observation Affects Reality" in the February 27, 1998, issue of *Science Daily*. In this study, they further discovered that "the greater the amount of 'watching,' the greater the observer's influence on what actually takes place." This ultimately says that the more attention we give to something with desire to influence through our emotions and our desires of the outcome, then the greater the effect.

Now this is exactly what I said previously in regard to Dr. Emoto's experiments with rice. It is the desire, intent, and clear instructions of the experimenter that have the most effect on the rice. Not just the pure emotion.

Science is only now starting to prove what we have already intuitively known for many thousands of years. As you will find in Buddhist philosophy and practice, the first verse of the Dhammapada is very telling.

All things are preceded by the mind, led by the mind, created by the mind.

—Dhammapada

It is purely your intentional focus that is your reality.

This is what Einstein referred to as "spooky action at a distance." The missing part to his relativity theory revolves around his lack of understanding on humanity's ability to connect *wholly* to the universe. As renowned physicist John Wheeler said, "We are not merely observers of the universe, we're participators in the universe, because every place we look with an expectation to find something, it is our expectation that will ensure we find something."

If it is your intentional focus that is your reality, then you will also find that your reality will be completely different to mine. In the end, is modern Western science just proving the reality of what that particular scientist is hoping to find? Don't we all simply just take what feels "right" to us to create our own reality and our own happiness? Why should you worry what other people's opinions are, because if they don't match what feels "right" to you, then you won't feel happy with the result. You will look for another answer until you find what looks and feels "right," until your view on the world is completely different from my view of the world. *Your* reality is *your* search for meaning to make *you* happy. Once you realize that, then altering your thoughts and emotions should make more sense.

It has been determined that faithfully envisioning and imagining and then adding emotional intention, especially when done in a group or in "mass," can create a reality.

Information from HeartMath, in the latest scientific research, shows that it has been realized that humans operate in coherence. As humans, we are composed of numerous interconnected networks of biological structures and processes. Coherence is the order, structure, harmony, and alignment within and among systems. These can be as small as atoms and organisms, or as large as social groups, planets, or galaxies. This means that every whole has a relationship with and is a part of a greater whole, which is in turn part of something greater. This means that you are not alone! Most surprisingly, physics has uncovered quantum coherence, which has given rise to the prediction of nonlocality and instantaneous communication between subatomic particles separated by vast distances. Does this mean that as more and more people learn how to handle their emotions, the more and more love energy we exude, and the more and more it strengthens and stabilizes mutually beneficial reality with each other and with Earth itself?

Imagine how a drop of water causing a ripple connects with other ripples from other drops of water to become a larger wave. Then it continues to converge with more and more ripples from other drops of water to then become an even larger wave. Now compare that to a thought energy wave and how similar thoughts can come together in coherence, forming an energy wave of higher amplitude, thus increasing the amount of energy carried by the wave. Increasing the energy of a thought wave has the potential to amplify its effect on matter, including not only your body and mind but your external environment as well.

Mahatma Gandhi once said, "Be the change you want to see in the world," and be that change coherently and watch the world change!

It makes you wonder about the origin of "Mass," where the religious will come together in worship. Similarly, hundreds of years ago, the Gregorian monks would sing in the Solfeggio harmonies in prayerful, hopeful love. A "Collective Consciousness."

This is exactly what scientists are now discovering. Take, for instance, the experiment by the Washington Crime Prevention unit with a group of 800–4,000 people in meditation over a period of two months in 1993. In this controlled scientific experiment, they found that the crime rate over that same period dropped by 23 percent. Interestingly, they also found that as they increased the group size, the rate of crime dropped in almost the same frequency.

Three years ago, I cut down on watching TV. I didn't turn it off, but I limited my watching. I still found myself addicted to the news. I would look for it on social media and get involved in the discussions. One year ago, I realized I was living other people's realities. I would listen to such comments as "This world is a terrible place," "What has the world come to?," "This didn't happen in my day," and "We aren't safe anymore." It seemed that humanity had completely forgotten about the previous two world wars and countless territorial fighting happening all over the world for centuries. It seemed it had slipped their minds to consider that to some people, the world wasn't safe back then, either. It just feels worse now, because it is in our face every day on the television and social media.

We watch it blaring in our lounge room, and worse than that, we welcome it in. We share it with our children and then say to them, "Oh goodness, look at the world you have to live in now."

The media have a saying that I want you to really think about: "If it bleeds, it leads." Why is it that the media think we want to see the bad stuff first? Or in some cases, *only* the bad things? Why is it that the media think that we need to hear about that one terrible thing that happened on the other side of the world, but we wouldn't care about the one million good things that our fellow human beings did that same day?

Let me tell you that in reality, humans on a whole are a wonderful species. We do wonderful things every day. There are people who make bad choices and do terrible things, but on the whole, we are amazing.

One year ago I withdrew from the news. I withdrew from TV unless it was a documentary that I could learn from. Some people tell me I live in a bubble. But I have the most amazing bubble with the most amazing view. My world is gorgeous! My world is loving! And my world is kind! I don't live in a world of fear or judgment. I simply live in a world where everything is possible, and everyone deserves a smile. People around me are happy, and if they aren't, they are simply having a bad day. That doesn't make them bad people. Everyone has a bad day.

My purpose in telling you this is to try to portray that your reality is what you make it. Your reality is your choice and only your choice. You can choose to get lost in other people's opinions and other people's dramas, or you can choose to be encased in your own happy world. Lead your life in love and kindness and just watch what type of world unfolds in front of your eyes.

If your emotions can control your reality, why on earth would you choose to feel angry, sad, frustrated, disappointed, or unforgiving—in essence an "inner hell"? If you want an amazing and happy reality, then it would make sense to consciously choose to vibrate in the emotions of happiness, love, kindness, joy, amusement, pride, and graciousness. Your inner heaven and sanctuary! ☀

The Best Defense against being hurt
is to feel good about yourself.
The way a person responds to
you or treats you
says more about them,
than it does about you.

— **BRENDA SHOSHANNA** —

Chapter 12
THE POWER OF JUDGMENT

When I was a first-time mother, I realized how harsh we, as a species, can be on others and ourselves. I was forty-one weeks pregnant, and my obstetrician looked me up and down and said, "I'm sorry to say, but you are never going to drop. We will need to cut that baby out." My obstetrician was an incredibly tactless man. He was an extremely funny man but didn't quite grasp the highly strung nature of an anxiety-driven, almost-new mum. I was booked in for a C-section one week later! I only had one week to prepare for a major surgery and the loss of the ability to try a natural birth. During that week, I came to terms with a lot of judgment on myself. I felt depressed that I couldn't have a baby naturally. My body just wasn't set up for it. I kept thinking that if I were a mother one hundred years ago, I wouldn't have even survived childbirth. I felt like a failure at being a woman. I felt the *judgment* that I *perceived* other woman would place on me for having a C-section. I felt the weight of a *judging culture* on my shoulders.

When my first baby was born, I held her perfectly shaped head and healthy little body in my arms and stared into her gloriously blue eyes, realizing that it didn't matter. We were both healthy, and we were both alive—and that was all that mattered to me.

However, even perceiving the judgment I would feel from other people still didn't prepare me for the onslaught of actual judgment that I did receive from a bunch of women who *did* look down on me for my "elective" Caesarian, despite a noncommittal baby not making an appearance on her own.

Being a new mum seemed like such a battle with judgment and hurt. And a lot of the harsh battles were in my own head, because of my own perceived guilt.

By the time my second baby was born, and being faced with the same problems of the first pregnancy, I had come to terms with judgment, and you will be happy to know that I no longer cared what anyone else thought of my second "elective C-section." By then I had come to terms with my own limitations.

Fear of judgment can stop us from performing our best in life. When I turned to energy healing, I feared what my friends would say about me. I feared how they would feel about my new endeavor. I actually stopped myself from following this dream for many years, due to my fear of judgment. Being an energy healer has been a secret longing of mine for many, many years—probably since my obsession with learning everything I could about life after death when I'd turned twelve years old. However, I had experienced so much judgment every time I had spoken my thoughts on these subjects that I simply stopped expressing my desire. I decided to "fit in."

Judgment is something we all have to deal with, and usually we are our own worst critics when we don't live up to our own expectations.

Judgment seems to stem from our cultural upbringing. I look at my children now and I remember when I was learning how to settle my toddler's tantrums. I was taught that to stop her from crying, I should distract her with a shiny toy or a change in location or a food treat. This just never felt right to me. I could tell that even after the distraction, she was still sad, and worse, she was confused about her feelings, and it was never resolved for her. I changed my approach a little later, and I would let her cry into my shoulder for as long as she liked. I would add a comforting *shhh* until she quieted, and then we would talk about her feelings. I didn't treat her like a baby, and instead I spoke to her like she was an adult. I would reassure her that it was okay to feel sad or angry, and I would then explain the reasons why she couldn't have the toy or why she needed to share. I would explain how the other person would be feeling, or I would explain the danger of what she was doing. Then I would tell her that it was okay to make mistakes, and that the main thing was not the mistake itself, but the lesson learned from it. If we can't learn from our mistakes and make amends to correct them, then we aren't growing as a person. Children don't always understand this the first, second, or even twentieth time you tell them, but eventually it does sink in.

Most people would look at me and wonder why I would speak to my toddler as if she were an adult, but my toddler would respond amazingly and grew into a well-adjusted child who knew her feelings and knew that if she was sad, she could talk about it with me, and we would look for the lesson to learn together.

Were you taught to help your sadness with distraction? Look at yourself now. When you are sad, do you head for the fridge? Do you head to the shops to buy something pretty for yourself? How does this make you feel? You may feel better temporarily, but does that feeling last long, or do you return back to sad and incomplete again soon after and look for something else you want or heard about? Maybe you buy a chocolate bar on the way home from work.

When we are young, distraction also teaches us that it's not okay to cry. It's not okay to feel sad, and it's not okay to voice that sadness. We grow up thinking we need to keep our emotions to ourselves. We grow up to be adults who don't feel anything. We become numb. We become desensitized. We see other kids stifling their tears, so we do the same. We see violence on TV and video games, and we think this is normal, so we don't feel for people who suffer violence. We are just glad that it wasn't us. We learn that our pain is to be controlled so as not to disturb anyone else. We forget our natural instinct to feel sympathy. When we forget sympathy, we learn selfishness. When we forget sympathy, we learn seclusion and then we learn loneliness.

When we are "alone," we have to rely on learning how to live through conformity. This is the safe route. If we just do what everyone else is doing, we should be okay. So that's when judgment rears its ugly head, and we wonder why someone isn't doing it the "right" way. The way that everyone else is doing it. We forget that there is no such thing as the "right" way. We are all simply the product of our own life choices, and we are never actually alone, because we are all connected with the one energy of love.

Dealing with your pain when you feel it is so important. Some pain will need to linger for a little while because things such as trauma, extreme heartbreak, and betrayal are devastating. Your body, mind, and spirit will all take time to heal from such trauma, but everyday nuances are important to nip in the bud before they become a bigger issue than they need to be and needlessly take over your consciousness.

If you can teach this to children when they are young, then you may have children who cry more than others, but they will be the ones to grow up knowing the healthy way to deal with their emotions. They won't be the ones suppressing their sadness with food, materialistic things, and suffering in silence, leaving them hurting their physical health as well as their mental and spiritual health.

They won't be searching for happiness outside themselves, because they will know that happiness comes from within. Happiness is created by the power of your consciousness to take your emotions head on and lead the charge up the emotional scale to vibrate at the frequency of love or above. They will know that completeness doesn't come from an outside source. Completeness is that journey within. ❁

STEP THREE:

Start

Chapter 13
THE POWER OF WRITING
YOUR THOUGHTS

The most important opinion that anyone can have is the one they have of themselves. If you believe you are a failure, then you will fail. If you believe you are creative, then you will make the most-amazing creations. If you believe that you aren't capable, then you will let fear stop you from achieving anything. If you believe you are a good writer, then you will write that book, blog post, or article that will leave everyone gasping for more.

Stop and listen to your thoughts for a minute. What are you telling yourself? We are constantly talking to ourselves throughout the day. Where are your thoughts on the emotional scale?

"Oh man, do I have to get up already?" "Why does that child never sleep in?" "Quick, we are running late again. We are always running late!" "What is that car doing?" "What a fool." "What is she wearing?" "What can I make for dinner?" "Nobody likes anything I cook; I'm not sure why I bother!"

We are seldom aware that we do this, but we have a running commentary going through our heads daily. So if you just stop and listen to yourself for a little while, you will start to hear how negative you actually can be.

All your thoughts have a measurable electrical output. In other words, your thoughts, just as your emotions, have their own energy. However, your thoughts are also magnetic. Your body parts have their own energy. All this energy combines to shine out your aura, matrix, or light. Your aura is the measurable energy output of your combined body, mind, and spirit. We will talk more about the aura later, but for now, let's concentrate on your thoughts, because it is the vital part of the process in consciously choosing to make a change.

The important thing is learning how to catch a negative emotion or thought and consciously knowing how to shift it immediately before it sets in and takes over.

To complain is "to express dissatisfaction, pain, uneasiness, censure, resentment, or grief." Complaining is when you will find fault with something that annoys you.

Complaining is the path away from happiness. Listen to what you say and think? Take a day, and attempt to take a step outside your body and observe just how much you complain or think negatively throughout the day.

You could have all the positive affirmations happening at the right times, but if in the next sentence you stop to complain about something, you lose all that good work. Complaining puts the lower emotional vibrations out into your energetic matrix and, therefore, will attract similar vibrations back in. This means you are gaining more things to complain about. The more you complain, the more annoying things find you. This is what some people refer to as Karma.

Take a moment to think about that!

Are you complaining daily? Are you complaining a lot daily? What do you complain about?

Simply becoming consciously aware of your complaining will help you vibrate at a higher frequency. Every time you complain, take the time to stop yourself. Take the time to think about how you can reword the sentence or thought to become a positive vibration instead. Take the time to be patient and realize that it isn't always about you, and that quite possibly whatever is happening has its own reason. Perhaps it is happening to teach you a new lesson in life. Just because it is annoying to you, take the time to ask yourself why you think that it is annoying. The most important thing to remember about complaining is that it is resisting the abundant energy flow. You will find that in general, people will complain about the things they lack. "I can't afford to pay the bills." "I don't have the energy for that!" "My car keeps breaking down; I need a new one."

Take the time to ask yourself how you can change your thinking so that you are allowing the abundant energy flow rather than resisting it.

What is a situation that you complain about? Does it get any better by complaining? Or does it seem to just get worse? By complaining you are simply focusing on it more. You are forgetting that where focus goes, energy flows. So instead, take the time to focus on the positives of the situation, and there are always positives. I see so many social media posts saying "I just need to vent." This is the belief that getting it all out will make things better. This is the hope we have deep down, to find out that we aren't alone. We are looking for sympathy, reassurance, and a sense that we belong to a community of people who think just like we do.

Psychologists say that some complaining can in fact be healthy. This is true if it is an instrumental complaint. This is one that expresses an unfair grievance that you have determined needs to corrected. If what you are upset about can be fixed, then complaining is legitimate and can be quite healing. This comes back to the F.A.S.T.R. emotions. Feel the pain, acknowledge the pain, and then start to take action to fix it. Your action might be to effectively complain to the person who can fix it. An example would be if you were having problems with someone at work. You might complain effectively to your employer about the issue, with suggestions on how to rectify the matter.

However, there is such a thing as a chronic complainer. These are the people we label as whiners. Or the people who are so negative that other people start avoiding them. Do you know someone like this? Perhaps it is you; perhaps it is a good friend.

So the next time you have a complaint, write it down. Sometimes that is enough to vent and release it to heal, rather than confessing this to someone else.

Once you have written a negative complaint down, tear up the paper or burn it, and let it go. Then rewrite your complaints into positive statements, bearing in mind that what you write will open the door to allow the same energy to flow back to you.

If you still feel the need to know you aren't alone in your thinking, then take it to your friends or your partner and try to word it so it isn't a complaint. Perhaps put it into a question. For example, "How can we encourage the kids to hang their towels up?" rather than "Oh my goodness, I hate it when the kids leave the towels on the floor; they are so filthy!" Can you see the difference?

Ultimately, effectively complaining is a great way to connect with other people. And connection is great. Releasing the grievance can be healing, but if it is something that nobody can fix, or relate to, please ask yourself if venting to someone else will serve any purpose other than to direct more energy into the problem. You want to release the complaint and let it go; you don't want to hang onto it until it eats you up inside.

This is where we use the A of my F.A.S.T.R. Process. This is where we acknowledge our pain and start objectively rationalizing and applying some logic to the situation.

Acknowledging isn't just accepting the pain; the literal meaning is to "accept or admit the existence of the pain and recognize the importance of that pain." We have discussed previously how important it is for you to feel the pain, and now it is time to give pain its farewell and good wishes by asking yourself to consciously think about the ways you can *start to heal.*

After you have been through my F.A.S.T.R. Process for the first few times, it will become a habit. It will become so easy to lift yourself up again and release pain. However, when you are in your low moments, when heartbreak and sadness are too much to bear, it can be a journey that takes time. It took me five to seven years after hitting rock bottom to completely learn how to forgive and then to heal. I stumbled through the dark by myself, and although I did get counseling, I still found that the tools given to heal were basic in explanation and didn't give the full picture. It is okay to take your time, but with these tools I teach you, and your perseverance to follow my advice, I hope you can heal and follow your path a lot faster than I did.

When you ask yourself the best way to heal, you talk to your heart. You reflect within. You listen to your intuition and you follow your light. This is the time to ignore the ego.

Writing things down with a good old-fashioned pen and paper can be so liberating to your soul. It is a very good form of release, and the ability to release and let go of negative energies is the key to expanding into happiness.

When you are so caught up in your pain, it is so hard to think straight. One minute you are thinking you will change your life completely, and then the next you are holding on to the "normality" of life, locked safely within your "comfort zone." Writing is one of the most powerful tools you have right now in among the pain and the rage, the reason being is that when you write it down, you begin to acknowledge the pain, and it starts to make sense. When you write it down, you begin to see the real problems and can then prioritize those problems more easily. It also allows you to put your deepest desires and the energies of those desires out into the universe. It allows you to get the anger out and bring the balance back in. It allows you to look back over it with a critical eye and realize what you like and don't like about your own thoughts. Writing it down brings the control back to you. It allows you to ask yourself how to change your current situation, which will in turn change your thoughts to be of a positive vibration. So write a letter to God. Write a letter to the pain. Write a letter to your ex. Write a letter to the person you are trying to forgive. Choose one or choose them all. Just write what comes to mind. It doesn't need to make sense; it just needs to come out. Then read it through and ask yourself what you should change to make your thoughts more positive. If you don't feel ready to read it straight away, that is fine, but come back to it every week until you do feel ready.

Free Intuitive Writing

Author Note: Make sure you have a pen and paper for this next section!

The next writing exercise is called the intuition exercise. Free intuitive writing comes from a deeper place within you. It is a message from the inner consciousness. It releases the voice of your unconscious intuition. It often helps to explain the source of intense emotional reactions that seem inappropriate or that you have trouble understanding.

What you need to do is to relax and try to empty your mind. After a few minutes of thinking of nothing, wait for something to pop into your head, and just write what comes. It doesn't have to be a list or in any order, just write wherever your pen leads you. Don't worry if it makes sense or not; simply write your thoughts. Let your hand write, and use the back of your mind or your heart to write what you hear or feel. Everything in this exercise is relevant. Capture every word and image that occurs to you, even if it embarrasses you. The main rule is to write fast and don't think about what you are doing; it doesn't need to make any sense.

Once you are done, you can now see your *Map of Consciousness*.

When I first did this exercise, I remember going blank, and it was like I had just woken up when I finished. The automatic writing just took over. I looked down to see a page full of writing and drawings, and some not necessarily relevant to what I was thinking or feeling at the time. However, when I look back on this first map of consciousness I can see the relevance of it in my life now. It all makes complete sense. It felt like I was writing my innermost desires and some things I had never even been aware of or even completely acknowledged myself, and I can say that it was almost a prediction of things to come for me.

Through participating in this intuition exercise, you should have realized quite a few self-truths, and you might have realized that through learning to talk to your Higher Self and listen to your heart, you can acknowledge your pain and the fact that you need to make a change. Once you allow yourself to acknowledge your pain, and you consciously decide to elevate your emotions, you can achieve anything you put your mind to. You have claimed back the power from your pain. ✺

Writing it down brings
the control back to you.

— LIZ BARALLON —

Chapter 14
THE POWER OF MANIFESTATION

Claiming back the power of control for your own thoughts and emotions brings to the forefront the realization that you control your own reality and, therefore, your own destiny.

Manifestation is a powerful word. It comes from the Latin word *manifestare*, meaning to "make public" or even to "make real."

There are three important things to remember in manifestation. Feel it, believe it, and attract it.

Emotions are your signals telling you to move away from something or move toward something. Your emotions are powerful in being your guides to happiness. And your happiness is to live a life you desire and deserve. When you desire a particular reality, you need to be able to feel the emotions of already having achieved that reality.

Belief requires you to expect your desired reality. It asks that you truly believe that your desired reality *can* and *will* happen.

Attracting your desired reality is what occurs once the other two factors are in place. With your combined emotions, desires, expectations, and belief, your overall frequency rises, allowing attraction of those same higher frequencies, in what is known as the Universal Law of Attraction.

The fundamental principle of the Law of Attraction is that "like attracts like." In the energetic world, this means that vibrations of similar frequency are drawn together. If you can imagine two droplets of water moving closer together, you know that they will eventually attract each other and join together to form a larger droplet. When we put that into the context of our intentional thoughts guiding the emotions to create a powerful electromagnetic frequency attracting similar frequencies, you can see how this law will work in your own manifestations.

The Law of Attraction states that if you focus on a thought or desire for at least seventeen uninterrupted seconds, it will activate the matching frequency. If you can extend that focus for over sixty-eight seconds, then that vibration can become powerful enough for manifestation to begin. Gradually as you increase your emotions and thoughts to your desired reality, then these thoughts become more and more consistent and eventually become habit.

I use and teach five magic words in the art of manifestation, and I call them the five magical A's.

Ask

When you realize that your reality is in your control and the Universal Law of Attraction is in charge of bringing it to you, you simply need to ask for what you want. Verbalize it, visualize it, and feel it.

In today's world of online shopping, I like to think of this as placing my order online for my desire. I put through the order, I pay for it, and I wait expectantly for that order to arrive in the mail.

Anticipate

Anticipation is half the fun. Most of the time, the most joy we experience is when we are waiting for the big day to arrive. It's like booking a holiday six months in advance. You plan all the details, buy all your clothes, look at all the activities you would like to do on the holiday, and you dream, visualize, and feel it every single day leading up to the actual event. That feeling of anticipation is so wonderful that it is almost better than the actual event.

So after you put your online order in for your desired reality, choose to feel the anticipation for it to occur. Look in your mailbox every day if you want to. Do you remember when you were a kid and you used to run to the mailbox every day in anticipation that a letter might be for you, or there might be a parcel with your name on it? Every day you would check the box, and every day that you didn't receive that parcel, you just waited until the next day to run out to the mailbox again in case that parcel arrived this day. Your anticipation for the parcel didn't dampen from the disappointment that it hadn't arrived yet. You simply had *faith* and the *belief* that it would come soon.

Already

Already is one of the most powerful words in the English language in regard to manifestation. It combines the words *all* and *ready*. Ready is defined as "denoting something that is available, suitable, or prepared for a particular use or purpose." And *all* is defined as "*completely*." Therefore, *already* means to be *completely available and prepared for your purpose*.

Already is what I refer to as a magic word. I use it in energy healings, and I use it in affirmations. It helps shut down resistance to the desired reality, opening up the pathway to manifestation.

Allow

Allow follows on from *already*. *Allowing* means to let go of the negative emotions and thoughts surrounding your desired reality, and to open yourself up to actually achieving it and succeeding. When you use the word *allow*, it feels almost like you unblock your energy channels to create an uninterrupted flow of similar energy flowing back. It also allows your thoughts and emotions to remain positive and shut down the lower thoughts and emotions quickly. You are finally starting to allow the abundance you deserve to flow into your life.

Appreciate

To appreciate something in your life is to completely understand, recognize, and enjoy the good things in your life. Appreciation is gratitude amped up, and the power of feeling gratitude is one of the most significant keys in the process of manifestation. ❂

*Be completely available
and prepared for your purpose.*

— LIZ BARALLON —

Chapter 15

THE POWER OF YOUR WHY AND SETTING YOUR GOALS

When you start to look for a way to figure out your desired reality or, as it is commonly referred to, your goals, you generally already have a good idea of what those goals might be. It may be a vague idea or simply an idea that will lead you into the general vicinity of where you want to be, or you could even be so specific that you know every single detail of what you want to achieve.

When coaches tell you to find your "why," are you left scrambling in wonder as to what on Earth they might be talking about?

A *why* is your *purpose*. It is your reason for getting up each morning to go to work, to pay the bills. It is the reason you keep going to work, even though you don't particularly enjoy your job. It is what you are working toward. Your one day when you have enough money, enough time, enough love, enough . . .

If you don't put that *why* into focus, you may end up flailing around accomplishing nothing in your life, stuck in a dead-end job, going nowhere, and simply working to pay bills, rinse, and repeat. You fall into the trap of distraction, which can be quite dangerous in not reaching your potential in both emotional guidance and life purpose. If you keep putting your dream off because you are distracted by the next pretty item you "need," then your dream will never come to fruition.

So how do you figure out your *why*? Possibly it is jumbled up in your head with no clear direction, or possibly you have no idea what it is, but you just have a sense of something pulling you along, or possibly you know exactly what it is, but everything you do seems to take you further away from it.

Whatever your why is, there are some clear and defined ways to figure it out and look within yourself to ascertain why it is so important to you.

When establishing your why, I would like you to think of three goals that you are hoping to achieve in your life. Think of your "One Day When"! What is it that you will do one day when you have enough money, or one day when you have enough time, or one day when you have the motivation? Choose three goals. At this point they can be big goals or little goals. They can be materialistic, like a house by the water, or they can be situational, like the perfect job, or they can be emotional, like being able to work from home.

Think about what makes *you* happiest in life, and pick your top three goals; then fill out the diagram that follows. Keep writing even if you repeat your answers. The information below will help you feel clear, focused, and more motivated to achieve your goals.

GOAL 1	GOAL 2	GOAL 3

_____ _____ _____

_____ _____ _____

| Why is this important? | Why is this important? | Why is this important? |

| Why is this important? | Why is this important? | Why is this important? |

| Why is this important? | Why is this important? | Why is this important? |

What emotions does this evoke? · What emotions does this evoke? · What emotions does this evoke?

_____ _____ _____

_____ _____ _____

_____ _____ _____

_____ _____ _____

You may ask why you need to start turning your why into a goal. Goals are an important motivator—especially if you feel overwhelmed by how much is going on at the moment, or you feel like you're lacking direction, or even if you have a big project to tackle. Whether you *achieve* your goals depends on whether you *start* to take the action needed. But what decides whether you take action in the first place? The answer is based on how motivated you are!

Is your WHY big enough to make you strive to reach it? How important is it to you to feel the emotions you are hoping to gain simply through attaining the goal you desire? Is your comfort zone really so good? Is the fear keeping you in your comfort zone really that scary? Or do you think that you could face it to finally reach the emotion and ultimately the reality you desire?

While working out your *why*, you probably went through a range of emotions and realized a little more about yourself than you knew previously. Maybe you have realized you have more courage than you thought possible, or maybe you have realized how important a stress-free life is to you.

A lot of the time when we think about goals, we think they need to be really big—and that can get overwhelming. To achieve the emotion you desire, maybe you need to change how you think about goals. A goal should be anything you want to do or achieve. This could be big, small, or even completely random.

Another way to ascertain what is important for you to do is to think about the things you really *don't* want in your life, and write these down. Determining what you don't like is the biggest help to realizing what it is you do want in your life. Once you have written down your list of the things you no longer want in your life, take a look at it. These thoughts are your resistance to abundance of your desired reality. Every time you think of something you don't want in your life, you are exuding the vibrational frequency of the emotion attached to the disappointment that it is in your life. The Law of Attraction doesn't differentiate the words if the attached emotion is of a lower frequency. It simply sends the same frequency back to you, which is why sometimes it feels like everything is going wrong. Now take that list and think about how you can turn these things around to become goals with positive emotions attached to the words. For example, you could turn "I don't want to be just another number in a large company" into "I want to be a valued member" or "I want to run my own business and treat my staff as valuable."

Goals can be made in many different areas of your life. When you are writing your lists, think about:

- Personal qualities
- Friendships/relationships
- Family
- Spirituality
- Work/study/career
- Physical health
- Interests/hobbies
- Attitudes

Have you heard of the term *your zone of genius*? This is the area where you excel. If you think about *you* right now, can you tell me the thing you do *really well*? What is it that you think is super easy, but everyone else always says: "I have no idea how you do that . . ." or "I couldn't do that!"

I like to refer to it as "Following Your Light." What lights you up inside? What makes you so happy or so relaxed, or so at ease when you do it? It could be swimming, writing, playing with children, looking after people, teaching—it could be anything.

I always look at my children's teachers and I tell them that I have no idea how they could work with kids every day. I personally think anyone who decides to work with children and teach them and play with them daily is a saint. I absolutely adore my children, but I think I would go crazy having to sit in a classroom of twenty children and maintain order. I, on the other hand, love teaching, but I will stick to teaching adults, I think.

Personally, I struggled throughout my life to figure out my zone of genius. I am a jack of all trades, and I enjoy doing a little bit of this or a little bit of that and creating this and problem-solving that. I remember doing a career personality test when I was in college studying massage. I was a little lost. I wasn't enjoying massage, and I had just left university having studied podiatry. I knew I wanted to heal, but nothing was sitting quite right with the things I was learning.

My results came back in from my personality test with only one option. I should be a referee. *A referee?* I didn't even play any sport that required a referee! I remember thinking that personality tests were a right proper waste of time. Who would tell someone that they should be a referee? Surely being a referee would come from having a passion for a particular sport they had been playing for years? So, from that result, I took away that I was fair and just and was able to look at both sides of every situation, which was a very big strength I already knew I'd possessed since I was very little. My ability to take a step out of the situation and look at it from both sides did absolutely distinguish me as very fair, but this wasn't something I wanted to pursue in my career—maybe as a mother, but not as a career.

I recently had my astrological chart done, and my astrologer was amazed. He told me I have 11 planets and stars in my 12th house when I was born. This means that just on the horizon rising up as I was born, I had a constellation party going on. Typically a planet or star in your 12th house will align with certain qualities and strengths you will have throughout life, and statistically it has been proven that those born with these 12th house attributes will typically go on to be successful in a career needing these strengths.

So when most people generally have 1 or 2 planets or stars in the 12th house, and I turn up with 11, I now realized why I lacked direction and considered myself a jack-of-all-trades. It was because I could enjoy many things and could go on to excel in any chosen field. My downfall was that I just couldn't decide which chosen field I wanted to try.

It took me a very long time to acknowledge that I wanted to write, and even then I put it off, thinking I wasn't good enough. It took me an even-longer time to acknowledge that I wanted to change people's lives through helping them to discover ways for the body to heal itself, through natural alternatives, such as coaching and emotional healing.

For fifteen years, after my last personality test, I avoided placing any emphasis on personality testing. I took the opportunity to do other tests in the hope that I wouldn't always be considered a good referee, but I found most of them generalized me into an introvert who was analytical. Which was true, but still no help in discovering my zone of genius.

My biggest help was to look within and discover the answers to the following questions. Take the time to write the answer to these questions yourself.

1. If I had all the time and money in the world, what would I be happiest doing?
2. What is one or two things that I find so easy and relaxing to do, that others struggle to do?

Think about what you have written. Is there a way that you can turn this into a career? Is there a way that you can turn this passion into a way to make money? When we choose something we love to do in return for money, we will no longer feel we *need* to work another day in our lives.

With all my displeasure in personality tests, I did find one I love. I would love to share it with you now. It is a free online test that you can find at www.16personalities.com.

It is a test that splits people into sixteen personalities based on how you interact with your environment; where you direct your mental energy; how you make decisions and cope with emotion; how you approach work, planning, and decision-making; and how confident you are in your abilities and decisions. I found my result of INFP-A, one of only 4 percent of the population to be extremely accurate for me. An INFP stands for Introversion (I), Intuition (N), Feeling (F), Perception. INFPs are considered to be the diplomatic mediator, and I quote: "INFPs have a talent for self-expression, revealing their beauty and their secrets through metaphors and fictional characters." Now you know why I always reference movies to make my point.

I think it will also help you to pinpoint your zone of genius, allowing you to see a path to follow your light.

Once you have determined your whys and set your mind on your desired reality, one of the best ways to start achieving these goals is to "chunk it down." If you can take what feels like a seemingly impossible goal now and establish smaller steps to get there, then you will be giving yourself a defined plan to follow and deadlines for each step. For instance, let's take the example of writing a book. First, I would need to decide what I wanted to focus on and to incorporate into the book. Then I would chunk it down into the important aspects and allocate chapters and the outline of what those chapters would include. Next, the deadline would be decided, telling when I would like to have the book finished. I would establish a time frame for each chapter and then allocate hours or word count each day to achieve those goals.

Now I have an actual plan to achieve my goal of writing my book. Each and every step will become an important milestone. It will be a small goal in itself, and one I focus on until I achieve it. I can then move my focus onto the next step. So now writing a book has gone from a whimsical dream to a set plan.

When creating smaller goals, it is important to celebrate those smaller goals. So the next step is to decide on your celebratory reward. Will it be a glass of wine or a piece of chocolate? Maybe it will be a dinner out or a movie. The reward is totally up to you, but once you achieve every small goal, make sure that you reward yourself so you can remember how far you have come, how good it feels, and how much better it will feel to accomplish your end goal. ❀

Every time you think of something
you don't want in your life,
you are exuding the vibrational
frequency attached to that thought.
These thoughts are your resistance
to the abundance of your
desired reality.

— LIZ BARALLON —

Chapter 16
THE POWER OF HIGHER EMOTIONAL AFFIRMATIONS

When deciding to change your thought process in order to achieve a desired reality or goal, a good method to begin with is listing the thoughts that you want to focus on. These are often described as affirmations or mantras.

An affirmation is defined as "the emotional action or process of affirming something and declaring it to be true." A mantra was originally used in Hinduism and Buddhism as a word or sound repeated to aid concentration in meditation. In Sanskrit it literally means "a thought behind speech or action," from the word "man," which in ancient Sanskrit origins means to "think," so it is, therefore, related to the mind.

A mantra is actually quite interesting because the om sound used in meditation is said to vibrate at 528 Hz—as is the "hahaha" in a laugh and the "ooooaaahhhwwww" of a yawn, and the "hhmmmm" of a sigh. As it turns out, we try to heal ourselves every day with a mantra.

For the purposes of what I am about to teach you, let's use the word "affirmation." It is important to remember that mantras have their place in our healing, but affirmations must use present-tense intentional thought, as well as harness all higher vibrational emotions to work to their best potential.

Common teachings over the last twenty or more years tackle the exercise of using affirmations to change your thinking around to be more positive. This teaching focuses on the belief that constantly thinking, saying, or singing positive-worded sentences will have higher vibrational energy attached to those words, which vibrate in your aura and attract situations or items of similar vibration to you. The idea is that you concentrate on simply repeating a positive thought over and over again until it becomes your reality.

However, if you have already tried affirmations, mantras, and positive thoughts, I'm sure you have already realized that these are often not effective on their own. This is simply because, as we have discussed in depth, if your emotional state isn't healthy and already in turmoil, which is where most people are in emotional health generally when they turn to affirmation training, then "positive thinking" is rarely able to produce a long-term shift of the negative emotions.

Previously, it was taught that emotions follow thought, meaning that if we simply change our thoughts, then we should be able to gain control over our emotions. However, recent studies have discovered that emotional processes operate much faster than thoughts, and they will frequently *skip past your reasoning process* to take on a life of their own. This means that your emotions commonly bias your thoughts beyond reasoning or logic.

Since thoughts and emotions can work separately in our system, it is important to try to have them work coherently to form the optimum electromagnetic frequency to obtain your desired reality. So how do we do this? First, we need to bring stability into the emotional system to bring peace and clarity to the mind. Having both systems in sync allows you to access your full range of potential to manifest your visions and goals. The ability to balance your emotions and align them more to happiness and above will allow your consciousness to gain more control over the process of manifestation.

Now we are ready to start the steps needed to process any emotional pain. Through the F.A.S.T.R. Process of feeling your pain, acknowledging that pain, and starting the process of elevating your emotions through intentional thought guidance, you should be starting to feel *hopeful* and a little more *content* in where you are emotionally right now. You might not be "happy" just yet, but you certainly have more good days than bad. You are willing to accept your circumstances, and you know that your only way to grow is to start working toward happiness.

With your emotions in a hopeful situation, you are ready to start affirmations. Now is the time that positive affirmations will work well for you. If you try affirmations when you are sad, or fearful, they will not be as productive or have the powerful manifestation you need. It may feel liberating to start with; however, because your emotions habitually come back to the lower vibrations, those liberating feelings won't last very long.

Your mind is a very powerful tool, and when you consciously choose the intent of changing thoughts, your mind will help you achieve anything you set yourself to do.

In the past, we were taught that the left and right sides of the brain think in different ways. Have you ever heard someone state that they are a "right-brained person"? The theory is that the left brain thinks in words, and the right brain thinks in pictures and feelings. Your right brain, therefore, should control the left side of the body and the nonverbal feelings of emotional and instinctive feelings. Right-brainers are said to be more spiritual and creative. The left brain, on the other hand, controls the right side of the body and thinks in a logical, reasoned, and ordered way. Left-brainers are said to be logical and analytical.

This, however, has been shown to be incorrect by Stephen Kosslyn and cognitive neuroscientist G. Wayne Miller in their book, *Top Brain, Bottom Brain: Surprising Insights into How You Think.* They tell us that science just doesn't support the left-brain, right-brain division. The fact is, we all have our talents, interests, and gifts. While it is true that the right-hand side of the brain physically controls the left side of the body and vice versa, and the speech and language center mostly exists in the left side of the brain, patterns cannot be determined where the whole left-brain network is more connected in some people or the whole right-brain network in others. Kosslyn and Miller introduce a brain that communicates in different modes: being a mover, perceiver, stimulator, and adaptor. Their book includes a test that you can do for yourself to understand your own dominant way of thinking.

What this all determines is that your personality is your fingerprint and individual to only you. But just because it is a series of electrical stimuli, it doesn't mean that you can't control it.

Negative thinking can stop all motivation and enthusiasm. When your emotions are low, your thoughts tend to also be low, and you begin to be hard on yourself and others. You stop seeing the good side of situations, and you focus too long on the bad side of them. It has been proven that people who are prone to worrying about external situations cannot carry out a task as well as those who might have the focus and determination to succeed in the task. If you are continually worrying that you might fail, your focus goes into all the different ways you might fail, and this has a tendency to become a self-fulfilling prophecy. On the other hand, if you replace this worry with positive motivation, then you will find that enthusiasm and hope for the outcome outweighs the fear of it going wrong. Positive thoughts enhance your motivation and your ability to think with more complexity to find the solutions to overcome any problem thrown your way.

A great way to determine your view on the world is to ask yourself if you are habitually an optimist or a pessimist. Optimistic people have a strong sense that everything will work out fine, no matter what goes wrong. They don't fall into a sense of hopelessness when faced with adversity, and they get up and try again to overcome any obstacle they might have failed at. A failure isn't their end destination. It is simply a reason to reassess and try another way. A pessimist, on the other hand, may just give up on a dream simply because they tried and failed. The failure then creates emotional pain and worry, and they simply don't believe in themselves *enough* to give it another go. *They just give up.*

If you have a tendency to be pessimistic or if you saw yourself in the description of a pessimist, I want you to look at what you gave up on. I want you to reassess the situation and determine if there is another way to give it another try. If there is, I want you to work up the courage to do it. Put your thoughts into action, and get yourself *trying*. Failure is simply a stepping stone to an amazing destination. The stepping stone isn't meant for sitting on. Get up and move.

Remember also that your pessimistic thoughts and negative thinking bring with them vibrational frequencies as well. They are electromagnetic frequencies looking for a similar partner in that situation. If you are negatively focusing your energy, you are attracting in more-negative situations.

Through visualization and motivational self-talk, you can negate any negative thoughts and words you might have, and the subsequent attached energy vibration. Remembering that your emotions run on a different system than your thoughts makes it important to feel the *right emotion* when you speak your new affirmations. Using these two methods coherently should produce magnificent results.

When you speak your affirmations, it is important to speak them in the first person, and as if the event or situation has *already* occurred. It is also vital to be specific and concentrate only on a few at a time. Feel free to dream big, but start the goals as stepping stones in order to get to the big dream. Once you reach your stepping stone, you can change your affirmation to suit the next stepping stone. Please don't forget your five magical A's. These five words of ask, anticipate, already, allow, and appreciate are words and signals that will produce the right emotions of excitement and happiness to open up the energy channels to more-powerful affirmations and, therefore, a better probability to attaining the desired reality.

In my experience, singing the affirmation has also produced amazing abundance quickly. This is because we usually evoke joy and happiness through signing a song we love. So adding an affirmation to your favorite tune can create instant happiness and joy along with the power of the new thought. Another tip is to add humor and laughter to your affirmation. Make your affirmation so wonderful that it makes you laugh.

As you say your affirmation, you want to be able to evoke the feeling of having accomplished that step. If you can feel how happy you would be to have already reached that goal, then you are evoking the right vibrational frequencies that you need to manifest it. You need to keep all your words positive. For example, let's look at the difference between these two sentences:

"I am grateful and happy to no longer be in debt"
as opposed to
"I am grateful and happy to be financially abundant."

The energy of your words forms no discrimination. If you say the word "debt," you vibrate at the energy level of "debt." On the other hand, if you say the words "financially abundant," then you will vibrate at the level of "financially abundant." So transform your affirmations to have uplifting and positive words.

Repeating the affirmation as many times as you can throughout the day will also help you cement it into your thought process. You will notice the more you say your affirmation, the more you feel the happy emotions associated with your desired situation, and the closer you are to believing it as truth.

In saying this, I know that sometimes when you are stating something that hasn't happened yet to be true, it can feel like you are lying. But the universe and your emotions don't feel this. It just feels the words and the intentional happiness you imagine and feel when you speak them. Your words vibrate at a higher frequency and attract similar situations with those frequencies and open doors to allow more good things to flow through to you.

Recording your affirmations onto your phone or a CD and listening to them frequently throughout the day—in the car or in the shower, etc.—can help you remember them and repeat them frequently. When you say your affirmations, you want to use an affirmative and commanding voice and repeat it at least three times. Sometimes, when I have really wanted to achieve a goal, I have repeated my affirmations one hundred times or more

Some examples of some affirmations and how you should say them are listed below:

I allow and appreciate feeling loved.

I appreciate feeling the frequency of the sound of love.

I allow the joy of already achieving my financial goals.

I appreciate leading an already successful team.

I love the anticipation of my booming business and the joy it brings.

I am joyful and appreciative that my family is already happy and healthy.

I ask to be consciously kind and loving to my family all day.

I allow the anticipation of experiencing a wonderful day.

I appreciate already feeling happy.

Abundance already flows to me on a daily basis.

I am allowing doors to open to wonderful things.

I allow conversations with my Higher Self whenever I want.

I appreciate that I can keep my promises.

I allow the joyful anticipation to strive for my goal weight.

I allow the changes I need to become happy.

I appreciate that I always give my best and remain positive.

I am already earning my goal income.

I appreciate that I have allowed myself to write and finish my book.

I ask and allow that I change my life for the better every day.

I appreciate that I am bringing up strong-minded and already emotionally stable children.

I allow amazing communication with my family.

I am already healed.

I am already healthy.

I am already happy.

I am already abundant.

My artwork is already famous.

I appreciate that I have already sold 1,000 copies of my book.

I allow the abundance of earning $10,000 monthly.

I am already the best recruiter in the company.

I already earn the largest bonuses at work.

I allow myself to feel the joy when my boss recognizes me for hard work.

I appreciate that I am driving the car of my dreams.

I am excited and appreciative to be working in my dream career. ❁

*Your mind is a very powerful tool,
and when you consciously choose
the intent of changing thoughts,
your mind will help you achieve
anything you set yourself to do.*

— LIZ BARALLON —

Chapter 17

THE POWER OF VISUALIZATION

To begin your affirmations, it is also wise to incorporate visualization techniques. I think sometimes we underestimate the importance of dreaming. Daydreaming is something we do as children. We live in our own wonderful fairy tale where anything is possible. We dream of being able to fly like a fairy, or to swim like a mermaid, or to have a beautiful ball gown like a princess. We dream of having x-ray vision or even having super strength to save the day. Our daydreams provide us with an escape from reality into a world where magic can happen.

I am one of those mothers who encourage magic. I love imagination and the stories that imagination can bring. When my children ask me if something is real, before I answer I will always question them on what they believe. If they think it is real, then I will agree and tell them that reality is what you make it. If my child still thinks fairies are real, then they are very real in her world. If your child still believes in Santa, then allow them to have the reality of the anticipation of Christmas Day, because that is their reality. To this day, I still believe in fairies. I still look on the ground, between the flowers, and peak through windows, hoping to glimpse a fairy flutter by. I watch every butterfly, and I wonder if it is really a fairy in disguise.

When did you lose that ability to dream? I guess when you were told not to be silly and that fairies don't exist. Unicorns are just a myth, and mermaids cannot be real. Someone squashed your dreams and told you that you were silly for even thinking it. They gave you a filter, and you had to reduce yourself to conformity again. You had to look around for the nearest "acceptable" belief and walk that path with the other nonimaginers, all the while secretly wishing you could be the one fluttering along on the other path in your own little land of dreams.

It may be wise to start looking for the next fork in the road and heading off the beaten track though, because a study by Guang Yue, an exercise psychologist, looked at brain patterns in weight lifters and found that the patterns activated when lifting hundreds of pounds were similarly activated when they *only imagined they were lifting*.

Visualization works in your brain through lighting up a pathway of neurons. If this pathway is used only once, it will fade away; however, if you keep using this pathway repeatedly in many visualizations of the same occurrence, then you will create a deep and permanent pathway that is hard to undo. It becomes *habitual*.

A famous sports study in basketball done by Australian psychologist Alan Richardson, called "Mental Practice: A Review & Discussion Parts 1 & 2," also found this same result. After initial skills testing, he split the subjects into three groups. One group would practice shooting goals for one hour every day for thirty days. The second group would visualize shooting goals for one hour every day for thirty days, and the third group did nothing. When he retested the group, he found that not surprisingly, group 1 had improved by 24 percent. He found that the third group, having done nothing for thirty days, of course, had showed no improvement at all. However, remarkably, he found the second visualizing group had improved by a whopping 23 percent.

When I was younger I would do this very thing. I was a tap dancer, and I loved it. School on the other hand, I found very boring, and I had a lot of issues concentrating on things that didn't interest me. So I would sit there and tap. I would imagine being on the stage with the spotlight on me, performing my solo to a packed audience. I would tap out my routine, counting to eight over and over again. I would improve in tap every day. In the end, there wasn't a tap step I couldn't do, because I had already practiced it for hours in my head.

There are many great visualization techniques, and the best way to start is to establish a highly specific goal. Imagine how you will feel when you achieve that goal. Visualize a mental "picture" of it, as if it were occurring to you right now. Put as much detail as you can into the "picture." Use all of your five senses to do this and think about the following:

Where are you? What do you hear?

Is there a smell? Something that you associate with success or fond memories perhaps?

Whom or what do you see?

Can you taste anything? Salt in the air? A great glass of champagne?

Is there a texture to your goal? What are you wearing? The grass beneath your feet? The steering wheel of your new car? How does it feel?

What emotions are you feeling right now?

Can you see the picture of your very own success in your mind's eye?

Can you almost reach out and touch it? Remember this feeling! This is the feeling we would like to harness and keep throughout the day.

Another visualization technique is a *Visualization Board*. If you don't already have one, please make this your priority. Write out your goals and search for visual representations on the internet or in magazines or your own photos. I like to incorporate quotes as well as specific pictures of things I am aspiring toward.

For example:

- A specific car. I have the Tesla pictured on my board.
- Search for the perfect house in the perfect location. Is it a farmhouse? Or a house on the water? Or a house in a particular estate? Or a unit in the city?
- Look for a picture of your idea of *love* if finding a romantic connection is a goal. Look for a picture of what you would imagine your ideal man or woman to be. Remember that it doesn't only have to be looks; it can be an attitude or a personality or a great parent or a good provider.
- Search for a picture of a family if you are hopeful for a family.
- Add a prayer or affirmation into your board.
- What about your career? Find pictures that depict your dream job.
- What about your spiritual growth? Find pictures that help you remember to always search for more and grow more.
- Think about exercise, weight management, meditation, flexibility, surgery, health, happiness, love, career, faith, anticipated income, or family. Try to think of everything and incorporate it all onto your vision board.

I print out all of my pictures and affirmations, I then laminate them all and place them onto a big piece of cardboard or canvas, and I hang it on my wall in my bedroom, at eye level when I am lying down in my bed. This is so it is the last thing I see as I go to sleep and the first thing that I see when I wake up. It helps me feel grateful and be hopeful each and every day. I urge you to do this as well. If placing it next to your bed makes you feel self-conscious, then place it somewhere such as your wardrobe or your personal bathroom, but make sure that it is somewhere that you will see it multiple times daily.

Another great technique is to write all of your affirmations onto Post-it Notes and place them around the house. I place them as a border around my bathroom mirror so that I can read them multiple times daily. Another great suggestion is to print out your affirmations on an A4 piece of paper and laminate the paper. You can then showcase your affirmations in your shower so that you can go through your visualization methods every time you take a shower.

If your goal is something that you can create in a smaller version—for example, a model of the car you want—why not go and buy or create that model and place it in a prominent place in your house. If it is something the whole family can benefit from, why not teach your partner and children this visualization technique and ask them to visualize owning it as well. The power of cohesion again will be very powerful.

Guided meditations are a great way to expand your visualization techniques. Below you will find the words to one of my guided meditations. Why not give it to a friend to read to you while you sit in quiet reflective meditation, and then swap and read it for your friend. It will help each of you understand your capabilities when you try both roles. ✿

Guided Meditation

Let's start.

Sit comfortably alone with silence, or with a peaceful, meditative track on. Preferably it would be in the chord of 528 Hz. Try the website Attuned Vibrations for some amazing music, all made with the Solfeggio harmonics chords.

Close your eyes and breathe deeply in and out a few times.

Now visualize a beautiful, bright bubble encasing you. Feel yourself floating in the bubble.

Now visualize a beautiful, bright bubble encasing the room or building you are in. These bubbles are there to protect you as you start to feel your energy.

Sit there for a few more moments, and listen to the silence or the music, and listen to your breath going in and out.

Visualize a bright light above your head. Imagine this light is love. Pure unconditional love. Source Love. Feel that love flow through you.

Feel the bright light shine down through the top of your head; feel it move into your forehead and down into your ears. Feel and see the light in your eyes. Now feel it move deep down into your throat and your shoulders. It travels down into your arms all the way down into your fingertips.

Feel the tingling sensation as the light of love fills your hands. Now the light moves back up your arms and into your chest. It fills your entire heart. Imagine the green of the grass and see that color flood into your chest and surround your heart. This is what love feels like.

Now feel the light turn back to bright and move into your belly and flood your core with light and love. Now it moves deep down into your hips and surrounding organs. It unclogs any energy blockages, and you feel at ease and free.

Now feel the light move farther into your legs, flooding your feet and toes with healing energy. Imagine that light moving fast toward the center of the Earth. Sending all your love and consciousness to Mother Earth and grounding you to your Base.

Imagine and visualize that Mother Earth sends that love right back up into you, and the bright light zooms up through the Earth, back into your feet and up your legs and into your core, and rests back at your heart. Feel all that energy burst through your heart and out to your hands to create a bubble of love.

Imagine your bubble. What does it look like? What color is it? Is it light or is it heavy? Can you see anything inside of it? Can you see words? Can you see pictures? Can you see someone?

Imagine the way you want to feel. What does that feel like? Push that feeling into your bubble. Imagine feeling so happy you can hardly contain your delight. Push that feeling into your bubble.

Imagine the affirmations that are important to you. Imagine writing them down in your bubble, slowly seeing and feeling each word. Push that affirmation into the bubble. How does it feel to have that wish come true?

Look at your bubble. Send it all your love and your light and ask that your bubble serve in guiding you forward. Now pull the bubble back into your body and into your chest. Feel the tingling as the bubble makes itself at home in your heart of unconditional love.

Now imagine yourself in a forest. It is green all around you. Trees and lush foliage surround you. Imagine that you have roots coming from out of your feet and growing down into the ground. Feel those roots reach the core of the Earth and then send the nutrients and minerals from the Earth right back into your body to ground you to the Earth again.

Send love and appreciation to the light source and open your eyes.

*Don't dim your light to accommodate
someone else's smallness.
We were all born to shine
BIG and BRIGHT!*

— LIZ BARALLON —

Chapter 18
THE POWER OF ASSERTIVENESS

It is so wonderful to have a plan of action that you can take to achieve your goals. Just that plan alone can help ease the chaos inside your head and draw in the right energy to create the focus needed to achieve the goal. Generally the goal and your perceived reward for that goal will also help push you along to face your fears and move you outside your comfort zone, but what if you are still scared?

Previously we have discussed the destructive power of fear, pain, negative thinking, complaining, and judgment. You now know the positive power of rising up and elevating your emotions to love, and you are feeling more confident, but is there still a certain part of you that feels scared to take action? Are you now second-guessing yourself and your abilities and contending with self-worth again?

Sometimes the first step need only be a small one, but it will require you to have some assertiveness. Once you start, it will become easier and easier, as long as you keep remembering that *failure is only a step toward growth.*

As you learn to become more assertive you will receive different reactions from different people, and sadly, not all of these reactions will make you want to jump for joy, but you need to keep remembering that you are changing your life for the better to attract the positive influences into your life and eliminate the negative influences.

Obstacles will come, of course. There is no avoiding them, unfortunately, but all you need to do is take a step back to look at the situation, and deal with the problem at hand as best as you can, remembering to act only in love and kindness as you would like someone to act toward you. There is a golden rule in being assertive, and that is to *always* make the other person feel important. If you can do this in a kind manner in any situation through compliments or thoughtfulness, then your desire will easily be accomplished.

Matthew 7:12

So in everything, do to others what you would have them do to you, for this sums up the Law and the Prophets.

If we take a look at the definition of assertiveness, it is to "state or affirm positively, assuredly, plainly, or strongly." We can easily liken this to our affirmations. Being positive about yourself and your wants is not so hard anymore, so expressing this to someone through making them feel just as important as you can have such a profound effect on both of you and any given situation you find yourself in.

Assertive behavior is that aspect of yourself that is concerned with saying, "I am worthy" and "I have just as much right as you." This can involve three insights:

1. Knowing what your rights are.
2. Taking action to do something about it.
3. Taking this action within the goal of attaining your emotional elevation.

Here are some things to think about when aiming to be more assertive in achieving your goals:

- Stop worrying about what other people think, or listening to people who are telling you that you should do it a certain way that you disagree with. *Take the control of your own life and become the master of your own destiny.* Your opinion of your actions is what matters the most.

- Luck won't arrive on your doorstep. Sure, our positive affirmations will help open up the doors of opportunity through pure electromagnetic energy, but you still need to be actively looking and searching for opportunities to help you achieve your desired goal. *Stop making excuses or blaming outside circumstances for your lack of success.* "If it is to be, it is up to me."

- Believe that you will achieve your goal. If you focus on things that will go wrong, then they will go wrong. Belief is your most powerful ally. Your ideas are great enough to become a reality. *Stop overexaggerating the abilities of others and underestimating your own abilities.* You are more than capable.

- Take a deep breath and give it a go. *Fearing judgment is a pointless waste of time*, because only *your* opinion matters in the situation of achieving your own goal.

- Focus, focus, focus. Pretend you are a torchlight and shine brightly on that goal. As James Redfield said, "*Where intention goes, energy flows.*" Give the situation your purposeful thought and stay true to your own desires.

- Control your thinking, and *don't let your thinking control you.* Hear your thoughts and rearrange them constantly to achieve that positive mindset that you need to really and truly believe that you are capable of attaining your goal. ✺

STEP FOUR:

Thank

Chapter 19
THE POWER OF GRATITUDE

In the Japanese language there is a term they use to express a sense of gratitude combined with a sincere desire to give back. It is the word *on*. It is a feeling of appreciation so strong that it stimulates a sense of wanting to pay it forward and share that feeling with the rest of the world.

The word "grateful" comes from the Latin term *gratus*, meaning "pleasing" or "agreeable." In these times, it means more than just this; it has a meaning of feeling deeply appreciative of any kindness. It is to be truly thankful so that it produces emotions of happiness and contentment.

Sometimes we forget to take the time to truly realize the amazing things that define our lives. This may be because often we concentrate on what we don't have rather than all the abundance we do enjoy. Consequently, our gratitude exists in perpetual conflict with our desire for more, whether we crave time, convenience, wealth, or enlightenment.

Science tells us that an "attitude of gratitude" is a good health choice. A grateful heart is a happy heart. I'm sure you have heard it before, but this is probably the most powerful way to overcome any pain you could be feeling right now. Simply being grateful for the little things will allow you to pinpoint the reasons you have to be happy, and concentrate on growing that happiness into a habit. If you are low, then you can start small. "I am grateful I could get out of bed today." "I am grateful that I am able to feel love." "I am grateful for the food I have to eat as soon as I wake." "I am grateful for a beautiful sunny/windy/rainy day."

Being grateful allows you to live in the moment. Too often we are in our own minds and tormenting ourselves over the past, or swimming in the future. We forget that our life is happening right now. It is called the "present" for a reason. It is a gift. Our life is what is happening around us. It is the kids sitting on the floor and playing, it is the cup of tea sitting beside you, it is the birds singing outside, and it is the dog panting beside you. It is being with those you love and doing the things you want to do. It is also doing the things you don't want to do, that you do for a good reason that is important to you. Look at the smile on your child's face. Did you not create that perfect being? Did you not clap the first time he smiled? Do you not rejoice in her happiness daily? Do you still love his smile, or do you take it for granted? Life is an experience, so don't waste precious moments taking it for granted.

It's time to start to appreciate what you already have. Take the time to look around and notice the little things, and why, or even how, their being around you will make you appreciate how loved you are. Look at the vase (or similar object) on the shelf. Who gave it to you? Was it someone who loved you, or was it a present from yourself? Do you even remember how you got it?

Gratitude is an attitude, a choice, and a habit. When we consciously practice being grateful for the people and situations around us, then by the simple law of "where intention goes, energy flows" we begin to attract better relationships and results. The habit of gratitude will be strengthened as you consciously make the choice to stop complaining and to be grateful each day.

There are many ways to remind you to feel gratitude each day. I say thank you out loud often throughout the day. I write it on the shower screen every time I have a shower. I also remember to say thank you every time my feet hit the floor when I get up in the morning.

I have a few bedtime rituals that help me remember to be grateful for my day before I sleep. Firstly, I choose one of my crystals, usually my quartz crystal because of its amazing healing qualities, and I put my thanks and wishful intentions into the crystal. I then place it under my pillow to infuse into me as I sleep.

Second, and most important, I write in my gratitude journal, and this is what I suggest everyone starts with. So I would like for you to grab yourself a diary, exercise book, or even a specially designed gratitude book.

In her program "The Mind Aware" and her book *Train Your Brain*, Dana Wilde teaches this particular setup in her gratitude journal. I have used it for years now and added a few changes of my own, and this is the layout that I recommend for you as well.

Gratitude Journal

On the first and left page at the top, write down the date and, beside it, put your dream salary. *Example: $10,000 a week.* Next, write down your accomplishments for the day.

Examples:
- Today I went for a thirty-minute walk.
- Today I spoke with twenty clients.
- Today I played three games with the kids.
- Today I read an inspirational book for fifteen minutes.

Next, write down your grateful list. No matter how boring or horrible the day was, you will always find something to be grateful for.

Examples:

- I appreciate the ability to feel love.
- I am grateful for two beautiful, healthy children.
- I am grateful for a wonderful partner.
- I am grateful to have supportive parents.
- I appreciate the recognition I received at work today.
- I am grateful for an amazingly fantastic relationship with my friend/partner.

Sign the bottom. By signing your list, you are acknowledging your control over the situation. You are acknowledging your ability to manifest more of what energy you put out into the universe. You are acknowledging your prayer.

On the second and right-side page, write a list of affirmations. This is the page to put all your hopes and dreams for the future. This is the page to pray. This is the page to put your thought energy out into your aura. This is the page to allow the electromagnetic power of your thoughts and emotions to attract similar electromagnetic vibrations back into your life.

Through practicing gratitude and affirmations daily, or at least when you can remember, you will allow yourself to live in the present and enjoy each moment. You will find yourself enjoying the small things that happen throughout the day more, and making a mental note to write that in your journal, so you will never forget it. You will live moment to moment and remember to enjoy life. Gratitude can provide so much happiness, and being thankful brings you so much closer to that feeling of love and happiness in your inner sanctuary. Remembering to feel gratitude every day elevates your emotions quickly to habitually stay above fear, anger, and disgust. Of course, you will fluctuate daily and have bad days. That's the beauty of being a human. However, the less time you dwell in the lower emotions, the better. The bad days are the most-important days to make the effort to try to write in your gratitude journal, because these are the habits that will bring you habitually back to happy.

When you are rising up from rock bottom or a tough situation, you are ultimately aiming to be able to thank the pain and the external situation for being the change you needed to guide you to the path you are about to take. As impossible as that may sound right now, you want to eventually be able to look back and say thank you to that situation, because without it happening, you would not have become as strong, aware, or as beautifully flawed as you are. 🌼

When someone is mean to you,
maybe it just means
that as souls, you both agreed
that they would teach you
a lesson of resilience.

— LIZ BARALLON —

Chapter 20

THE POWER OF
THE LESSON TO BE LEARNED

In the F.A.S.T.R. Process, you have now learned the importance of feeling your emotional pain in order to acknowledge the emotion, then to ask your higher self the best way to grow and move toward healing and releasing the pain. You learned how to start becoming aware of your consciousness in order to change your thinking, in order to elevate your emotions. You discovered how to recognize and stop negative thoughts, and to turn these around to become more positive. Then you learned about gratitude and the power it can have in bringing you back into the realization of what you have right now.

Throughout your spiritual journey you will encounter the three stages of *awakening*, *ascending*, and *enlightenment*. Awakening is that time in life when you realize that there is a fundamental truth that love can only be found within. Ascending is the journey you take up the emotional scale, and enlightenment is the realization that everything truly does happen for a reason, and usually it will serve the purpose of teaching you that you really can manifest a reality you desire.

Some people say that we choose to come to Earth each lifetime for an experience in connection, and that we choose a lesson to learn each time in order to allow our souls to grow and ascend toward more wisdom and become truly one with Source. There are cycles within cycles, and when on Earth you must learn that every experience holds a lesson to be learned that will allow you to grow and climb further up the emotional scale to a habitual frequency.

To truly know the importance of the "T" in the F.A.S.T.R. Process, you must not only *appreciate* your life and your present situation, but you must learn how to *thank* any emotional pain for helping you become what you have become. You are going to learn how to *appreciate* how far you have come, and what you have learned, now that your eyes are wide open and no longer shut. Without that pain, you would not be here. You would not be on this new positive journey into achieving your dreams.

Holistically, we are made up of three parts—the Body, the Mind, and the Spirit—and in order to create emotional change to consistently vibrate at happiness and above, you need to consciously elevate your emotions through consistent, conscious change of your thinking. Once you start to achieve this, you can start to understand the importance of your Spirit or Higher Self to feel the higher emotions of real love and real kindness and the importance of habitually leading your life in this way. Healing your body will then follow in the *release* section of the F.A.S.T.R. Process, as your body is purely the physical representation of what is going on with the other elements that make up your *whole.*

In the Bible, an interesting thing to note is that the Hebrew version describes the "Holy Spirit" as Ruach HaKodesh. This generally refers to the inspiration through which attuned individuals perceive and channel God or the Divine through action, writing, or speech. The "Holy Spirit" is often described in the Bible prior to a prophetic vision. This indicates that prophets channel their Holy Spirit in order to deliver their prophetic message. The fantastic thing is that channeling your Holy Spirit isn't confined to prophets. Prophets are merely the people who realized they could talk to Holy Spirit prior to other people. Everyone is capable of Ruach HaKodesh. It is within all of us, and *enlightenment* is your path to understanding your Holy Spirit. *The Holy Spirit is your Higher Self.*

Perhaps humanity has lost their way over the last few hundred—or even thousands of—years in referring to "channeling" as witchcraft, fantasy, occult, and hocus-pocus. Perhaps the truth has been hidden in plain sight all this time.

The defining aspect is the intent behind the channeling. Stuck in the darkness of fear and anger, channeling could manifest more negative energies and more darkness, whereas following the path toward enlightenment, channeling would manifest the divine light of love and happiness and knowledge of the truth.

Reaching enlightenment is about learning to thank your choices throughout life and to look back in reflection and realize that your winding path was for a specific reason each time. You will come to a point where you can pinpoint exactly what you've learned and where it's led or leads you. Enlightenment is your chance to thank your Higher Self for the lessons you have learned, and the experiences you have had.

It might sound crazy to you right now to think of a given negative external situation and entertain the thought of thanking it and showing any kind of gratitude for such an event happening. However, healing the pain comes with a gratitude for whom you have become. It comes with a gratitude for the strength you now have and a gratitude for the hindsight that allows you the lesson of how to better yourself with each and every obstacle.

Eventually, you come to a point in life where any obstacle will cause you to skip the worry and stress straight away and immediately look for the lesson you need to learn, and the best course of action you need to take in order to overcome the pain quickly and make the most of the situation. That is what the gratitude of the lesson gives you. ❁

STEP FIVE:

Release

Chapter 21

THE POWER OF
YOUR CHAKRAS

Previously we have discussed the importance of our heart in our intuition with its ability to detect external energetic stimuli, prior to the event actually occurring. We have also discussed the importance of the pineal gland in processing that external information to relay it to our consciousness and physical body, so that it is also known as our third eye. We have also just discussed how at microscopic level through our mitochondria, we are even perhaps energetic intuition working in symbiosis with each other, the Earth, and the universe through that powerful coherence that we have discussed.

If you can imagine your body to have energy centers, much like a radio that receives different types of frequencies to play different stations, you will be close to imagining how your chakras work. The chakras are the energy centers of our body. We also have over 720,000 *nadi* in our entity. The *nadi* is a Sanskrit word meaning "tube" or "pipe," and these *nadi* function like receivers and transformers of the various forms of *prana*. The Hindu *prana* or Chinese *Qi* (Chi) is considered to be our "vital life breath"—perhaps the oxygen we breathe, energized with the frequency of 528 Hz. It is through the *nadi* that this vital Chi energy is absorbed and transformed into the specific frequencies needed by the various areas of our physical body for sustenance and development. Most *nadi* are extremely small and play a minor role in your energy system.

The *nadi* connect to our major conductors for this energy. These conductors are known as energy centers and are called chakras. *Chakra* is the Sanskrit word for "wheels of light." There are seven major chakra centers plus many, many more minor ones. Through these centers we take in and send out the energetic vibrations of our personal thoughts, emotions, consciousness, physical being, and spiritual being. There are also approximately forty secondary chakras that are of significance; these are located in your spleen, the back of your neck, the palms of your hands, and the soles of your feet.

Your *aura* or *energetic matrix* is the representation of the different energy of all these aspects. Looking at this energetic representation of our whole person allows us to see what is going on intimately. Many people can see auras, and it is widely known and celebrated that everyone has the capability to see these energetic matrixes, but because most cultures are brought up thinking it is supernatural, occultist, or fantasy, then those gifted with the sight will tune out of that visual reality in favor of a more accepted reality. Many people can train to see these energies, and many people are born with the ability to see them already and simply need to fine-tune their gifts in order to understand what they can see.

Each chakra center in the body has a color association, and each color also has a particular vibrational frequency.

Here is a basic overview of each of the major seven chakras and what types of energy they relate to.

Chakra Overview

If you can imagine a drop of water landing into a pool and the circles of ripples that it creates, then you may start to understand the ripple of energy flowing throughout your body. In fact, it is this very same ripple effect, generally referred to as the fabric of space-time, that scientists have found in the universe. Imagine *gravity* is your drop of water and the space and time ripple of the fabric is your energy flow coming in waves. In a similar way the chakra centers are the gravity points where the drops of energy flow out to create an energetic ripple of different vibrational frequencies represented as color emanating from your body.

In ancient times they likened this ripple effect of energy to the lotus flower opening. I find both representations to be a fantastic way to describe the energy waves flowing out from your chakras at each frequency point. The energy is a directional flow, similar to the Fibonacci spiral, and you will find that each chakra has it's own direction for flow.

For simplicity, we will only explore the seven primary chakras here. The seven chakras are directly responsible for our physical, emotional, and spiritual health.

If the chakras are unbalanced, or present with blockages, then they will manifest in the physical body as emotional stress and illness.

The chakras have their own frequencies,

Depiction of the ripple pattern of each chakra point.
Image created © Liz Barallon with base photo
© AVIcons | istockphoto

and keeping these frequencies balanced and in harmony is essential in order for you to function properly. When your chakra frequencies are in harmony, you will feel connected with yourself *and* others. When you are "out of tune" and your chakras are "off balance," many problems can arise. Things that might seem trivial, such as a change in weather, stress, or even a sudden bump, are enough to throw your energetic balance out.

Scientific tests show that unpleasant sounds actually increase our blood pressure, pulse, and respiratory rates. On the flip side, sound frequencies can also have a positive effect on us, and we can stimulate each chakra individually by listening to its own special frequency in music. Incorporating the use of the particular chakra frequencies is the most direct form of chakra balancing and stimulation.

1. Root Chakra

Location: base of the body at the perineum

Color: red

Key: C

Solfeggio frequency: UT 396 Hz

F.A.S.T.R.: Situation

The first chakra is the Root Chakra. It is traditionally called the Muladhara Chakra, and is known as "I am." This chakra is associated with the sense of smell. It is located in the base of the body at the perineum and corresponds to your adrenal cortex glands. It is mainly associated with your survival instincts, grounding to Earth, your physical energy, and your self-preservation. Emotional issues housed in the first chakra are usually related to security, financial situations, manifestation blockages, trust, and fear. The Root Chakra vibrates to key of C and is associated with the color red.

In the F.A.S.T.R. Process the Root Chakra relates to the *situation* creating your emotional distress. It relates to the *fall*.

2. Sacral Chakra

Location: just below your navel in the pelvic area

Color: orange

Key: D

Solfeggio frequency: RE 417 Hz

F.A.S.T.R.: Feel

The second chakra is the Sacral Chakra. It is traditionally called the Svadhistana Chakra, and is known as "I feel." This chakra is associated with the sense of taste. It is located just below your navel in the pelvic area and governs the sexual organs: ovaries or testicles, bladder, bowel, and lower intestine. Your sexual energy and life force is here. Emotional issues in the area, to name only a few, are sexuality, creativity, shame, and guilt. The sacral vibrates to key of D and is associated with the color orange.

The Sacral Chakra relates to the "F" in the F.A.S.T.R. Process. This is your need to feel the pain.

3. Solar Plexus Chakra

Location: above your navel
Color: yellow
Key: E
Solfeggio frequency: MI 528 Hz
F.A.S.T.R.: Acknowledge

The third chakra is the Solar Plexus Chakra. It is traditionally known as the Manipura Chakra, and is known as "I do." It is associated with the sense of sight. This chakra is located above your navel in what you know as your core. It corresponds to your pancreas and governs digestion, the stomach, upper intestines, upper back, and upper spine. Your inner power and mastery of inner self are housed here. Emotional issues such as anger, power, intellect, assertiveness, aggressiveness, and self-esteem are found here. The solar plexus vibrates to the key of E and is associated with the color yellow.

The Solar Plexus Chakra relates to the "A" in the F.A.S.T.R. Process. It is the acknowledgment of the emotional pain.

4. Heart Chakra

Location: center of your chest
Color: green
Key: F
Solfeggio frequency: FA 639 Hz
F.A.S.T.R.: Start

The fourth chakra is the Heart Chakra. It is traditionally known as the Anahata Chakra, and is known as "I love." It is associated with the sense of touch. This chakra is located in the center of your chest and corresponds to the heart and thymus and immune system. Love, compassion, and unconditional love are here. Emotional issues found here are grief, relationship problems, and love. The heart vibrates to the key of F and is associated with the color green.

The Sacral Chakra relates to the "S" of the F.A.S.T.R. Process. This is starting the action to change.

5. Throat Chakra

Location: throat
Color: indigo/purple
Key: A
Solfeggio frequency: SOL 741 Hz
F.A.S.T.R.: Thank

The fifth chakra is the Throat Chakra. It is traditionally known as the Vishuddha Chakra and is known as "I speak." It is associated with the sense of hearing. This chakra is located at your throat and corresponds to the thyroid, the respiratory system, and metabolism. The Throat Chakra governs the throat, thyroid, mouth, teeth, tongue, and jaw and rules your self-expression and talking. It is associated with communication. Some of the emotional issues are fear of verbalizing your thoughts and holding expressions of joy. The throat vibrates to the key of G and is associated with the color blue.

The Throat Chakra relates to the "T" of the F.A.S.T.R. Process. It is the ability to thank the situation for initiating the growth.

6. Brow Chakra

Location: between the two eyebrows
Color: green
Key: A
Solfeggio frequency: LA 852 Hz
F.A.S.T.R.: Release

The sixth chakra is the Brow Chakra. It is traditionally known as the Ajna Chakr, and is known as "I see." It is associated with the sense of Mind. This chakra is also known as the Third Eye and is located between the two eyebrows, and corresponds to the pineal and pituitary gland. It is associated with hormones and growth. It also governs the skull, eyes, brain, nervous system, and all five senses. An imbalance in this chakra can present with emotional imbalances, poor intuition, depression, and hormonal imbalance. Your psychic abilities and imagination are associated with this chakra, all allowing yourself to be completely in the present, which is a main function of this chakra. The Brow Chakra vibrates to the key of A and is associated with the color indigo/purple.

The Brow Chakra relates to the "R" of the F.A.S.T.R. Process. This is the ability to release the pain entirely and evolve to consciousness of thought energy.

7. Crown Chakra

Location: top of head

Color: white or gold

Key: B

Solfeggio frequency: TI 963 Hz

F.A.S.T.R.: Becomes habitual

The seventh chakra is the Crown Chakra. It is traditionally known as the Sahasrara Chakra and is known as "I understand." Associated with the sense of Pure Consciousness, this chakra is located at the top of the head and corresponds to the pineal gland and central nervous system. It governs the top of the spinal cord, brain stem, pain center, and nerves and is your connection to the Source. An imbalance here can manifest in prejudices, judgment, and inability to see the bigger picture. When it is balanced, there is a deeper understanding of your spirituality and an awareness of oneness. The crown vibrates to the key of B and is associated with the color white or gold.

The Crown Chakra relates to the ability to habitually go through the F.A.S.T.R. Process each time you find pain, in order to habitually vibrate at the frequency of happiness and above. The Crown Charka is your wisdom attained through the process.

Chakras create the color of our Aura, and the energy that flows in and out of the chakras nourishes your DNA and the cells within your body with vital energy and the particular frequency needed for optimum health. To simplify this as best I can, imagine the chakra system as an energy transformer taking the higher frequencies of energy and condensing them down to lower-density frequencies that can be seen with our physical eyes. Some people have a greater visual capacity to "see" with their third eye and, therefore, can see more of the higher subtler energy. They will quite literally be able to see more frequencies than the average person, and that's why these people can see Auras.

When we speak of vibrating in the lower frequencies, you can see that we are more rooted to the ground. We are vibrating in the Root, Sacral, and Solar Plexus Chakras. These are the colors of red, orange, yellow, and a mix of these colors, which is a murky-brown color. If you look back at the emotional scale, you will notice how the frequencies of the colors also correlate with the frequencies of the emotions.

If raising your vibrations to happiness and above is what you have decided is important to achieve, then you need to be focusing on yellow to then acknowledge and accept your choice to move up the scale and resonate at love or above. The colors of green, blue, purple, and then white are your higher frequencies and also correlate with the higher emotions that you should be aiming to feel.

The more balanced each chakra is, the better you feel emotionally and physically. Further to this, the higher your emotional frequencies are, the more balanced your chakra colors become.

When you consciously choose to elevate your emotions through guiding your thoughts, you will produce the higher frequencies needed to obtain a greater infusion and balance of the higher colors. It is important to be balanced in each chakra, as each center has its vital functions. When any of these chakras become blocked or imbalanced, it invariably affects the others and the rest of the body, causing illness dis-ease, depression, and other emotional problems. Similar to working your way up the emotional scale through *Feeling, Acknowledging, Starting, Thanking,* and *Releasing,* you will also work your way up the chakra lineage, balancing each point in order to balance the whole. This is because you cannot be balanced in the Heart Chakra without being balanced in the Sacral Chakra. Through working through your emotions and aiming for the higher frequencies, you also work through your chakras to balance each one.

We also have another important energy center through what we call our energetic heart. This is in the same place as our Heart Chakra, but as we have discussed already, the heart holds a special function in being your intuitive receiver. It sits along your energy meridians and acts as an electrical generator creating an electromagnetic energy flow. This flow is a spherical-shaped flow of life force energy that constantly moves in all directions surrounding your body. It is known as the *tube torus* and generates the frequency and flow of your energy.

The field in which this energy flows is called the *toroidal field* and is essentially your container for your spirit. As you clear blockages from your energy points, this field becomes larger and expands.

When our chakra and energetic heart system are balanced we feel happy and healthy. It is clear to see that maintaining balanced energy flow through the chakras makes it possible to keep physical dis-ease and emotional di-stress away.

Other than conscious emotional control, there are many methods for balancing the chakras. These include crystal healing, color and sound therapy, essential oil healing, meditation, chakra balancing, guided meditations, Reiki therapy, splankna therapy, physical exercise, yoga, tai chi, and Chigong.

In the following chapters we will discuss a few of these and how you can help heal yourself through performing your very own energy healings and using other natural alternatives.

The toroidal energy field around your body. © Russiangal | Dreamstime.com

Your individual search for
inner happiness is the
meaning of your life.

— LIZ BARALLON —

Chapter 22
THE POWER OF MEDITATION

Sometimes, all you need is to just quiet your mind. When you quiet your mind, you silence your ego, and you allow for your Higher Self to communicate with ease.

All you need to do to quiet your mind is to simply close your eyes and intend to stop thinking and talking to yourself, while gently pushing away from your mind all images and emotions in order to find stillness to both body and mind. It is not about trying to force anything, but rather about inviting silence and peace into your mind. When you are first starting, it is likely your brain will like to choose this very moment to tell you that you forgot to wash the dishes, but simply try to observe the thought and not to engage in it. Visualize the thought moving away to wait until you have had your quiet moment.

Practice makes perfect, so try this exercise for five minutes a day to start with, and it will soon become much easier. Aiming for at least fifteen minutes a day will bring ease and comfort, as well as a greater ability for manifestation of your desires.

When you are meditating you are allowing positive abundance energy to flow, rather than resisting it with thoughts of self-sabotage. If you are thinking of nothing, you are putting your spirit into a neutral and balanced state, which helps bring more balance into your life.

The benefits of meditation are almost infinite. I could probably write a whole book on the benefits of meditation alone. From decreasing your stress and anxiety to increasing your intelligence, there are numerous studies and testimonials to prove the overall health benefits to quieting the mind and meditating for a little while each day. However, this chapter will focus on the correlation between meditation and uplifting and elevating your emotions.

Research has shown that people who practice the technique of transcendental meditation activate the frontal lobe of the brain, which affects the structural and functional connections between the different brain areas. This allows for more coherence and leads into better emotional stability and less of the lower emotions, like anxiety and stress.

Meditation allows for time alone with your intuition and Higher Self, which can help answer and solve a lot of problems. It has been proven to improve stress levels and increase happiness and self-awareness. It allows for personal acceptance and has even been proven to slow down the aging process. I'm still not sure why this isn't implemented into every school program, because this is a life lesson we should all be given.

While in meditation, the importance lies in reflection. In the quiet of your mind, your Whole Self comes together to reflect inward on your past emotions, attitudes, and actions and to come up with solutions to improve and metamorphose into a habitually happy person. And the best thing is this happens almost unconsciously during a meditation session.

To teach you how to meditate, I would recommend that you find a qualified teacher or a fantastic online program.

I teach a hand position that is focused on opening the midpoint of the chakras that connects the Heart and Solar Plexus Chakras. This is because through my research I have found that the vibration of love is found at the crossover point between the seven chakras. If you look inside the human body, you will find that the tracheal tube runs down from the neck to the heart, and then it branches off and leads to the two lungs. The lungs hold your breath. They hold your chi, which is your life energy. They are very important in connecting to your Higher Self, which is part of the chi.

Chi can be condensed down into basic terms to be simply oxygen. Perhaps we should ponder if our true Source is the seeds that produce the plants and trees that produce our life energy of chi? Perhaps our Source and our God are actually oxygen, or more succinctly, perhaps our Source is the Universal Consciousness of light and love frequencies carried within oxygen. Without trees, we can't live, we can't eat, and we can't breathe. Without oxygen, we can't live, we can't eat, and we can't breathe. Energy is carried in oxygen. Oxygen is a part of water. If water molecules can take on and reflect the vibration of our thoughts and feelings, wouldn't that mean that oxygen can take the vibration of our thoughts and feelings too? Are we just downloading information from oxygen?

Water has some beautiful correlations. As the waves of the ocean ebb and flow, so do our emotions. Sometimes waves seem to have a mind of their own, just as our emotions do, and the word "emotion" actually comes from the Latin word meaning to "move out."

Water also has a reflection. To move from the lower emotions to the higher emotions, we must reflect on our thoughts, emotions, and actions in order to cross over to light. There is no better way to reflect on our life, actions, thoughts, and emotions than in the quiet of the mind breathing in Chi during meditation.

Meditation is so good for both body and mind, simply because once you can ascend in your mind and cross over to the light side of truth being the happier emotions, you will find healing within the body. So your physical pain will follow your emotional pain, and your physical health will follow your emotional health. Meditation speeds up the process of reflection and ascension up the emotional scale and, therefore, speeds the healing of your physical pain as well.

I suggest you sit comfortably cross-legged, but I find meditation works well lying down as well. The important thing is that you focus on the Chi entering your body and filling your whole being with light, love, and truth. The Chi listens and reflects your emotions, helping you become one with the vibration of love.

If you would like to try sound healing with your meditation, I recommend a particular chant. I teach that the correct sound of *om* can be found through sounding the vibrational hum of the kiss within. You know, that sound you make as you air-kiss someone, just prior to the puckering squelchy sound. When I was taught meditation, I could never figure out the correct pitch to *om*. I was taught to look for a vibration within my head, or sound a different word, such as Thoth, but this one instruction allowed me to get the sound right finally. My *om*s were always too low as compared to making the sound of kissing in, so I hope this description can help you too. How appropriate that the *om* is really the kiss of love inside. It's a kiss to your Self.

Step 1. *Release the sound of the om and its vibration to start the meditation.*

Step 2. *Focus on breath and your inner happiness as you take deep breaths.*

Step 3. *Quiet and focus on your life and the inner reflection on changing what you can change and accepting that which you cannot. Focus on changing that which no longer makes you happy so you can focus on that which will make you happy. Focus on the truth that happiness is within us.*

Step 4. *Forgive and release judgment upon yourself and put your emotional pain into a bubble and send it away.*

Source is the
Universal Consciousness
of light and love frequencies
carried within oxygen.

— LIZ BARALLON —

Chapter 23
THE POWER OF
CHAKRA BALANCING

There are two forms of energy healing that I would like to tell you about: Reiki healing and chakra balancing. As an energy therapist, I incorporate both these healings into one, and I add a sound and crystal healing to help with a powerful energetic cleanse and balance.

A Reiki healing should really be performed by a correctly activated practitioner, and the healing given by Reiki healers can be profoundly life changing. I highly recommend that you find a local practitioner and visit them on a six-weekly basis.

In between visits, though, you can perform your own energy healings, as you should aim to make cleansing your energy a daily habit.

A chakra cleanse and balance are essential to help you nourish your body with positively charged energy. I have heard of many different ways to open and cleanse your chakras, including visualizing a flower opening around your chakra points or imagining color filling each area of the chosen chakra.

Below I have included a self-guided chakra cleanse for you to follow. If you add some healing music and treat it similarly to a meditation where you sit or lie in a comfortable position with your hands in the diamond shape connecting your heart to your Solar Plexus Chakras, then you will be in a fantastic position to receive the healing. If your hands become tired, simply place them on your thighs so as not to block the cleansing process of the chakras.

As instructed before, with the previous meditation, you may want to enlist the help of a friend to read this to you as you relax, and then swap so you can both benefit from a chakra cleanse and balance, or you can record your own voice reading this out loud and then play it while you also play your music and relax.

I have provided a link to this meditation on my website for free. This might be an option you might like to utilize. (www.lizbarallon.com)

Guided Meditation

Sit comfortably, alone with silence, or with a peaceful, meditative track on. Preferably it would be in the chord of 528 Hz. Try the website Attuned Vibrations for some amazing music all made with the Solfeggio harmonics chords.

Close your eyes and breathe deeply in and out a few times. Now visualize a beautiful white bubble encasing you. Feel yourself floating in the bubble. Now visualize a beautiful white bubble encasing the room or building you are in. These bubbles serve to protect you as you start to feel your energy. Sit there for a few more moments and listen to the silence, or the music, and hear your breath go in and out.

Visualize a bright white light above your head. Imagine this light is love. Pure unconditional love. Feel that love flow through you.

Imagine the white light flow through your body right down to your feet. When it reaches your feet, imagine the light to turn to a bright red light. Move the light slowly up your legs, helping it circulate over any sore places in your feet, knees, or legs. Bring the red light up into your groin area and into your Base Chakra at the bottom of your spine. Imagine the red light flooding this area with intentional love and grace. See the vibration of the red light come out of your Base Chakra smoothly. Visualize any blockages being dispersed. Project it both forward and backward from your Base Chakra as far as you can imagine, and then create the circle of red light around your Base Chakra.

Bring the light up and watch as it turns to orange. A brilliant orange light, the color of an orange. Flood your reproductive organs and kidneys with orange light and stop at any sore or problem areas. Flood your large intestines with orange light and come to rest at the Sacral Chakra. See the vibration of the orange light come out of your Sacral Chakra smoothly. Visualize any blockages being dispersed. Project it both forward and backward from your sacral chakra as far as you can imagine, and then create the circle of orange light around your sacral chakra.

Bring the light up and watch as it turns to yellow. A brilliant yellow light, the color of a sunflower. Flood your stomach and small intestines with yellow light, stop at any sore or problem areas, and come to rest at the Solar Plexus Chakra. See the vibration of the yellow light come out of your Solar Plexus Chakra smoothly. Visualize any blockages being dispersed. Project it both forward and backward from your Solar Plexus Chakra as far as you can imagine, and then create the circle of yellow light around your Solar Plexus Chakra.

Bring the light up and watch as it turns to green. A brilliant green light, the color of grass. Flood your lungs and your heart with green light, stop at any sore or problem areas, and come to rest at the Heart Chakra. See the vibration of the green light come out of your Heart Chakra smoothly. Visualize any blockages being dispersed. Project it both forward and backward from your Heart Chakra as far as you can imagine, and then create the circle of green light around your Heart Chakra.

Bring the light up and watch as it turns to blue. A brilliant blue light, the color of the daytime sky. Flood your throat, shoulders, chin, and mouth with blue light, stop at any sore or problem areas, and come to rest at the throat chakra. See the vibration of the blue light come out of your Throat Chakra smoothly. Visualize any blockages being dispersed. Project it both forward and backward from your Throat Chakra as far as you can imagine, and then create the circle of blue light around your Throat Chakra.

Bring the light up and watch as it turns to indigo. A brilliant dark purple, blue light, the color of the night sky. Flood your eyes, ears, nose, pineal gland, and brain with indigo light and stop at any sore or problem areas, then come to rest at the Third-Eye Chakra. See the vibration of the indigo light come out of your Third-Eye Chakra smoothly. Visualize any blockages being dispersed. Project it both forward and backward from your Third-Eye Chakra as far as you can imagine, and then create the circle of indigo light around your Third-Eye Chakra.

Bring the light up and watch as it turns to white. A brilliant white light, the color of a lamb. Flood your top brain and crown with white light and stop at any sore or problem areas, then come to rest at the Crown Chakra. See the vibration of the white light come out of your Crown Chakra smoothly. Visualize any blockages being dispersed. Project it up and around from your Crown Chakra as far as you can imagine. Imagine it to be like a halo of white light encircling your head, and then create the circle of white light around your Crown Chakra.

Now bring that white light down through the entirety of the chakras to cleanse and heal any forgotten spots. When all colors of light are mixed they form white light. This means that white is the most healing color you can visualize flowing through your body.

Send all your love and your thanks to the Chi energy and ground yourself by imagining yourself in a forest. It is green all around you. Trees and lush foliage surround you. Now visualize roots coming out of your feet and growing down into the ground. Feel those roots reach the core of the Earth and then send the nutrients and minerals from the Earth right back into your body to ground you to the Earth again. Send love and thanks to the light source and slowly open your eyes.

In completing a chakra cleanse, you will feel more energized and be left with a feeling of calmness and happiness as you begin your transformation into balance. ⚙

A chakra cleanse will help you feel more energized and you will be left with a feeling of calmness and happiness as you begin your transformation into balance.

— LIZ BARALLON —

Chapter 24
THE POWER OF CHI

I would love to explain to you a few things through my research and what has become individual interpretation of many things I have uncovered in this book.

Chi is the Qi in traditional Chinese theory, meaning "vital breath." It literally translates as breath, air, or gas. When I write Chi, I really mean oxygen. It is all around us and within us all at the same time. It gives us life and creates life and the very water we drink. Oxygen, like water, carries the energy of thoughts and feelings, making knowledge truly downloadable from the air that surrounds us.

It is the reason we feel amazing in nature, among trees, and around water. It is the reason we desire clean air to breathe and fresh water to drink.

A tree or plant releases oxygen. "We cannot live without trees." "We need oxygen to survive." "Take ten deep breaths, and you will feel better—immediately."

Trees and plants come from seeds. I look at the word "seed" and I think "life." A seed gives life to trees and plants. Trees and plants give life to creatures on Earth. A seed is, therefore, our source of life.

Water is created by the trees and plants through condensation, which is yet another reason why we need trees. Water also contains oxygen. When we drink water (drinkable oxygen), we feel revitalized and refreshed and we also need water to actually keep on living.

Let's, for a moment, look at the makeup of a molecule of oxygen. You need two atoms of oxygen to make up one molecule of oxygen. Each oxygen atom shares two electrons with the other, which makes it a double bond. Together they have sixteen

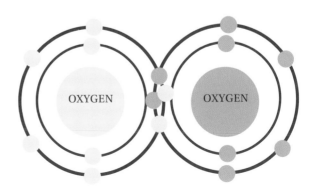

The bond of an oxygen molecule.
© Liz Barallon

electrons, and they unite as one. They live in symbiosis with each other. They need each other to create life.

It is known that 0.9 percent of the Sun's mass is oxygen, 49.2 percent of the Earth's crust is oxygen, and 23.1 percent of the air we breathe is oxygen.

Here is the downside to oxygen. Oxygen is very reactive. This means it is able to react with our cells in order to help them function, but unfortunately, the very thing we need to live is also slowly killing us. As we breathe in oxygen, we suffer oxidative stress. Our cells literally rust. Oxygen is what ages us, and oxidative stress has been linked to many illnesses; however, it is my theory that oxygen only leads to this effect of the oxidative stress that leads to illness when we live in the lower emotions of fear, stress, anxiety, pain, anger, frustration, jealousy, nonforgiveness, and judgment. It is the energy of these emotions that causes a physical misfiring somehow within the body. It is shown that people with clinical depression have less serotonin in their bodies. The general way to fix this imbalance is to give the patient serotonin-increasing drugs. However, what if it were actually the other way around? What if it is the constant lower-frequency emotions that are causing the serotonin to decrease, which in turn affects the nerve cells' ability to actually transfer any emotional energy?

In that case, depression should also be treated holistically through coaching processes such as this F.A.S.T.R. Process along with the medication to help clinically diagnosed depression. Without that generation of the habit of happiness, the body can never fully recover.

This lower emotional-frequency habit is an ingrained cultural teaching. These are the very things that as a culture we are taught to live in permanently. This is the importance of breaking free of the bindings that we place on ourselves and, therefore, living a habitually happier life.

When you start to rewire your brain to think in this way, you can understand how coherence affects us more than we could have imagined previously. If the majority of the world's population is taught to hide their emotions and live in judgment, then these thoughts are transferred to the oxygen around us. This then electromagnifies the oxygen with negative energy. We all hear people say that the world is so negative at the moment. There is a negative energy around. This is the very reason why this is true. This is also the reason why we need to change the energy around us to be more positive. We need to download happier, caring, and kind thoughts into the oxygen we breathe and walk through. Because oxygen is catching. Try to think of your negative thoughts and emotions like airborne viruses and bacteria. The negative energy around us is poisoning our oxygen. The oxygen is not functioning at its optimum capacity, and when we breathe it in and drink it in water, our bodies cannot use it to its full potential, and that's what causes the free radicals to increase and attack our cells.

If every single one of us can do our own small part and make the conscious decision to change our thoughts and thereby change our emotions, then together humanity can make a difference to not only the world and humanity, but to the collective health of all humanity. ❁

If every single one of us can do our own small part and make the conscious decision to change our thoughts and thereby change our emotions, then together humanity can make a difference to not only the world and humanity, but to the collective health of all humanity.

— LIZ BARALLON —

Chapter 25
THE POWER OF ENERGY HEALING

Reiki Healing

As discussed in the chapter about the benefits of balancing your chakras, the light that shines within and around your body is called your aura. When the chakras are unbalanced or blocked, they mingle with each other to create different colors. They will change daily according your thoughts and emotions of the day. There are different analyses of the different colors on the internet, but being close to someone who can actually see auras has allowed me to understand more of this fascinating aspect to our lives.

Red relates to the lower emotions of anger and betrayal. It also relates to sickness and the physical hurt of the body. It is often a color of people who are stuck in the practicality of their lives and live in anxiety and tension. Red can be a very important color to focus on keeping balanced. Cellular disease can originate with a blockage here. This can be cancer, or viruses and bacterial illness, and even genetic disease. Red is our root to the Earth and, therefore, one of our most important chakras.

Orange relates to feelings of low self-worthiness. It relates to a lack of confidence and fear and to being able to feel emotions. It also relates to the physical ailments of the large intestine, kidneys, and sexual organs.

Yellow relates to strength and acceptance. It relates to the acknowledgment of our emotions. It gives us the truth that we need to face our fears head-on in order to overcome and release pain. It is our chakra for inner reflection and the desire to overcome obstacles. It also relates to issues with the small intestines and the stomach and digestive tract.

Green is love and truth. Green is the crossover point for ascension, and it relates to the action we take to overcome the fear and pain we have suffered through life. Green displays the ability to listen more to your intuition. It is the halfway mark where you realize that action in love is now required. It relates to the heart and the lungs and the tracheal.

Blue relates to communication and living the truth. It means living in kindness and being kind to yourself and releasing all that no longer serves you. The blue relates to the gratitude that we feel through life, and the ability to learn from our mistakes and look for deeper lessons within everything that comes our way. It relates to the fact that sometimes we keep things bottled up inside, and this only serves to build up the pain. So blue is the initiation of the release of this pain when balanced and being used correctly. It relates to the throat, the voice, the mouth, and the ears.

Purple relates to vision and light. It means living aware of the importance of intuition and the ability to hear and listen to it more. Purple can allow divine release of pain and the ability to let it go completely. It allows you to see the bigger purpose in everything that happens and in everything that you do. Purple is ascension, and it rules the eyes, the pineal gland and the emotional connections, and frontal lobe of the brain.

White, silver, or gold relate to divine light. This is for the ascended. This means that you are living one with love and light and you know how to bounce back to your inner happiness very easily. It rules everything, because when all the balanced colors of light are mixed together, you get white light.

When the colors are murky or mixed without balance, it can mean confusion and blockages of some sort in the holistic, energetic body.

Healing, cleaning, and clearing the energetic aura or matrix are very beneficial. As I explained in the last chapter, a lot of our physical ailments occur through the energetic being or spiritual first. Our uncontrolled lower thoughts and emotions create a spin in our energy, which then affects us physically as we breathe it in.

A Reiki healing is beneficial in cleansing and clearing the chakras in order to maintain a balance to the union of the *whole* body.

Historically, Dr. Mikao Usui, a Japanese Buddhist monk, invented Reiki in the mid-1800s. While teaching, he was asked by a student how Jesus performed his healings, which sparked an interest to figure this out for himself.

Usui started a traveling journey in search of an answer, and when in the mountains of Kori Yama, he meditated for three weeks trying to raise his higher senses to find an answer. Just as he was about to give up, he felt and saw the vision of the divine light.

Usui then started a journey of healing and went on to learn that healing through Reiki was actually a two-way street, and the person being healed needed to do the inner work that goes along with that healing.

When you are initiated into becoming a Reiki healer, you receive an energetic activation with a Japanese symbol and are taught the techniques and theory behind the healing.

I remember quite vividly my activation into Reiki and the powerful visual experience I had. I opened my eyes to a place of bright light. It felt like a room so bright that it was like being in snow. I felt many light beings looking at me, and one crouched down and put his hands on my knees and said, "We've been waiting for you." I felt so welcomed and loved in that instant that I didn't want it to end.

Reiki to me is a feeling of contentment and relaxation. It is a moment that allows the client quiet reflection while many methods of energy healing can take place. Going to a Reiki practitioner, who will do the healing for you, is absolutely without a doubt the best way to heal the energy, simply because it allows you that quiet moment to notice the signs and signals as well as the emotions brought up to reflect upon in order to start the healing process, while not having to think and visualize with intent the light cleansing yourself.

The important thing to remember in Reiki is the *Oath*:

Just for today, I will let go of anger.

Just for today, I will let go of worry.

Just for today, I will give thanks for my many blessings.

Just for today, I will do my work honestly.

Just for today, I will be kind to my neighbor and every living thing.

—Usui Mikao

In *Ashati* Reiki, which is my lineage of Reiki, we learn all of the *Levels of Consciousness*. We teach that the root, sacral, and Solar Plexus Chakras are the Lower Consciousness linked through the Heart Chakra to the Higher Consciousness of the Throat, Third-Eye, and Crown Chakras.

If we look into the level of consciousness theory further, we can see that the yellow of the Solar Plexus Chakra is important as the top of the lower consciousness. It is the divine golden light of reflection within. The Heart Chakra is the color green of chlorophyll, and it is the middle colors in the visible color spectrum and the green of love and truth. It is the stepping stone to Higher Consciousness. The point between the solar Plexus Chakra and the Heart Chakra is the crossover point. Then, moving upward, we see the upper three chakras are of the higher consciousness as you ascend toward the healing white light of the Crown Chakra.

In a professional Reiki treatment, you will notice that a lot of the time, the practitioner will not touch you with his or her hands. This is because when the hands are held at a distance it can be much easier to feel the energy between the body and the hands if they are not touching. Personally, I have experienced both *hands-on* Reiki healing and *hands-off* Reiki healing, and I was left feeling disappointed from the hands-on therapy. This was because the feeling of touch actually took away from the energetic feelings I normally receive in a hands-off healing.

During a hands-off Reiki healing, a client can feel a variety of signals of the energy flowing from practitioner to client. They can feel tingles within their body. They may feel hot or cold. Many of my clients have reported the feeling of floating or of their body twisting. There seems to be a common feeling of being really heavy or really light. Many clients also report having visual experiences, such as swirls of color or seeing a rainbow. I have even had a few report feeling like someone was holding their hand or that they had visions of loved ones who had passed over. More commonly, clients tell me that they feel a tug on a source of pain—almost like I have reached down into their body and pulled out the pain. All these energetic feelings, without actually touching a client, can be quite humbling, while at the same time opening your eyes to the real possibilities of energetic healing. So please do go and see a professional Reiki therapist at least every six weeks. Your doctor will help you physically, but who helps you emotionally and spiritually? Reiki is one the best complementary modalities that you can try, because you are made of body, mind, and spirit. What you are physically feeling usually stems from what you feel emotionally, or worse, what you have blocked energetically. Reiki clears and cleanses in order to aid the physical and emotional healing.

Reiki is intentionally contacting Source or Chi, along with the client's Higher Self and asking them to give you permission to heal the client. Once permission is granted then the healing will occur, with or without the practitioner's intentional thoughts. All the practitioner needs to do is simply be the conduit for the Divine Light to flood into the chakras.

During the session the energies of the practitioner and the client become close enough for the practitioner to feel or hear messages. For instance I may feel a pain in my right eye to indicate that the client is suffering headaches around the right eye at the moment. Or I may feel sad and want to cry, which indicates that the client is in an emotionally sad place and needs inner love and support. Usually, as I start my Heart Chakra cleansing, I will hear messages about the client that I need to give. These are things that the client's Higher Self or guides wishes the client to work on. Often I will understand the fears that the client will need to face in order to move forward. I will get insights into the chakras that are blocked and need extra attention, and I will be able to advise accordingly.

A treatment feels like a wonderful glowing radiance that flows through and around you. You can physically feel the vibrations we spoke of earlier, or you might simply feel nothing at all. The healing will occur regardless of how you feel throughout the healing.

You will often find that any thoughts or emotions that arise will actually be coming to the surface for a reason, and you should take the time to acknowledge the sign that you are given and release it. This is your time of reflection, so any issues that do arise are usually the emotional blockages stopping you from proceeding in your journey up the emotional scale. But most of all, you should relax and enjoy it.

Reiki is a simple, natural, and safe method of energy healing and self-improvement that everyone can benefit from. It is a complementary therapy, meaning that it is to be done alongside any treatment provided by your doctor.

In between Reiki appointments, you will want to be able to help yourself improve energetically as well. Following, I will teach you some tips in performing your very own self-Reiki treatment.

In a Reiki self-healing, it becomes tiring to hold your hands above the chakra points, so it is advised just to lay your hands one over the top of the other to form a V shape on top of each point as you heal.

When giving yourself a Reiki Healing it is important to remember the three important aspects of *intention*, *love*, and *light*.

Hand position for a self-energy healing.

Your hands become your tools to channel Divine Light to the individual chakras. In Reiki you intentionally visualize divine white, purple, or golden light filling each chakra and moving that light around the area of the chakra in question. The choice of color depends on what you feel more comfortable with or what your intuition tells you is the right color to use.

To start, you will need to get yourself into a comfortable position in a quiet place. You can either sit or lie down. You will always need to energetically protect yourself. You can do this by setting up a crystal protection grid, or simply envisioning your white, safe, happy bubble of light surrounding you. Then you envision a bigger white, safe, happy bubble of light surrounding the room or the house you are in. You can do this through mentally drawing a big bubble around you, or some people visualize the house and visualize a bubble around it.

After you are energetically safe, then you place your hands, one on top of the other, in a V shape over your Crown Chakra; intentionally contact Chi and ask for the Divine Healing light. With love, feel and visualize the light flooding through your whole body through your Crown Chakra. Stay here for about five minutes.

Then you will move down to the Third-Eye Chakra and do the same thing. With the Third-Eye Chakra there are two positions. One is to place one hand on the middle of your forehead and one hand on the back of your head opposite the other hand. The second position is cupping your hands over each ear. Spend five minutes in each position.

Spend five minutes on the remaining chakras with your hands in the V shape, remembering to send intentional healing love and light to each area around each chakra.

When you reach the Base Chakra, you place your hands either over your groin or one hand on each upper thigh, on either side of the groin, to give the healing.

When you have finished, ground yourself through envisioning yourself in a forest, and while you are standing in that forest, imagine treelike roots travel down your body and emerge right into the ground. These roots reach down to the center of the Earth. Now imagine that the Earth sends those roots right back up to you, filling you with her minerals and nutrients and love.

Open your eyes and you are now finished your Reiki healing.

Crystal Healing

One of the first moments I remember being drawn to spiritual healing was when I was a teenager, and I felt energetically pulled into a crystal shop. I remember the feeling of coming home as I walked in. The smell and the crystals had this amazing energy that attracted me instantly. I was drawn to a citrine for clarity, and I remember having that crystal for a very long time.

What I didn't know back then was that crystals have this amazing power of absorbing, reflecting, and amplifying the energy. Quartz crystals create their very own frequency of energy. So much so that they are even used in all of our technology, such as phones, watches, and computers. It is important to note that quartz and many of the healing crystals used during chakra cleansing are made up of molecules of oxygen. This may help you understand how the crystals can then absorb your energy and share their own energy.

It is quite interesting to note that quartz crystals also have their own auras and can take on the color of the user. By using the crystals in a cleansing energetic healing, you can amplify the results of the healing through the properties of the crystals.

There are so many amazing crystals for you to choose from, and the best thing to do is to choose the one you feel most attracted to, or choose one that will help with the particular challenge you are facing in life. But in general, if you are looking to heal particular chakras, then the following suggestions would be a great start.

CHAKRA	CRYSTAL
Crown Chakra	Clear Quartz
Third-Eye Chakra	Amethyst
Throat Chakra	Lapis Lazuli or Sodolite
Heart Chakra	Green Quartz or Rose Quartz
Solar Plexus Chakra	Citrine
Sacral Chakra	Carnelian
Base (Root) Chakra	Hematite or Red Quartz

I recommend placing the correct-colored stone on each chakra point during a chakra cleanse or an energy healing for an amplified healing. I also don't go anywhere without wearing my chosen crystal for the day. At present I am not going anywhere without my clear quartz. I wear my chosen stone in an interchangeable rope necklace, but I have heard of other people carrying theirs in their purse or pocket or stuffed into a bra, if a woman.

Essential-Oil Healing

There is no end to the benefits of essential oils. They have been used for thousands upon thousands of years for healing, balms, cleaning, and practically anything you can think of. Most essential oils come from plants and trees and, therefore, come from and are infused with oxygen.

I cannot emphasize enough how *essential* it is for you to use essential oils in everything you do and to replace as many chemicals from your home with amazing oils that "bring light" to your body and spirit. Look for quality brands with more purity.

Sound Healing

The harmony of song is very healing. I have already provided much evidence on this fact. Whether or not 528 Hz is the sound of love or the sound of healing, it is definitely a sound you want to listen to often. The sound of 528 Hz allows your DNA to unravel and absorb more healing energy. So when sound healing is used in conjunction with energetic healings, the effects can be profound.

Throughout the course of your day, you naturally use sound healing to balance your energy. The frequency of love can be heard in the wind as it gushes by through the leaves of the trees, in the waterfall as you sit there in tranquility, in the sound of the waves, in the hum of a song, in the *shhhh* of a parent's voice, in your laugh, in your yawn, in your sigh, in your whisper, in a cat's purr, in a dog's pant, or in the sound of rain.

There are many other methods of sound healing, including the crystal bowl or the "signing bowls" healing. This involves the playing of many different-sized pure crystal bowls to create an amazing healing sensation.

I personally use tuning forks in my healings. I strike the 528 Hz fork over the crystals on each chakra point, which creates a powerful vibration for healing.

During your meditations, I recommend a beautiful piece of relaxing music playing. There are many albums around that offer the scientifically based healing tones. There are specific Reiki albums that you can get, and I have always found them to be very effective. And of course head to the Attuned Vibrations website for an album of the Solfeggio harmonic tones.

Self-Hypnotherapy

One of the most powerful tools I have found to develop my intuition was to listen to self-hypnosis tracks as I fell asleep. This is a great tool designed to unlock hidden potentials and memories stuck in the unconscious brain, to help the listener improve in many areas. It is also great at helping implant positive thoughts into the unconscious mind, which help make these thoughts a reality in your own head. Self-hypnotherapy is a great way to help heal your thoughts while your energy is being healed.

Hypnotherapy is also an amazing experience when performed by professional hypnotherapists, who have this innate ability to help you overcome blocks that you are having difficulty shifting. So if elevating your emotions is something you want to do, but you are finding there is a blockage that you are having trouble overcoming, or a blockage from something you don't even remember, then a hypnotherapist can help you with this.

A hypnotherapist can also help you to quit smoking, and as you have probably already figured out, if you smoke, then your lungs are not in great shape, and you are not making the most of your oxygen and Chi in order to create the best effort at elevating your emotions.

Divine Energy

In New Age Spirituality, we talk of this Divine Energy, but just what is it?

I'm not sure that anyone really knows for sure, as there are always many different theories and opinions. Commonly it is told that Divine Energy is universal light. It is thought to be the Creator light and love and energetic frequency that it holds. When we draw on Divine light and love, we draw from the Universal Consciousness.

Your emotions are electrical impulses, and your thoughts are magnetic impulses that come together to form an electromagnetic resonance. That electromagnetic resonance is your consciousness. The aim of the F.A.S.T.R. Process is to control the electromagnetic resonance through using the thoughts to guide the emotions. Once there is control, a certain balance takes effect and we move up the scale in vibration. The next step is to then become reunited with Higher Self and the higher vibratory dimensions to become united with Universal Consciousness in the Holy Trinity of *Source, Physical Body, and Higher Self*—also known as *the Father, the Son*, and *the Holy Spirit*.

In this theory, the Universe might have been started by something much smaller than the Big Bang. Instead of a big explosion, there was a union in oxygen to join the electromagnetic frequencies of emotion and thought, and they then developed into consciousness. When love occurs, our instant desire is to replicate or reproduce. Love is also a vibration of a frequency. Maybe, just maybe, it is the ultimate vibration that created us all. Maybe we were all created with the vibrational frequency of love.

The Father, the Son, and the Holy Spirit. Source, the Body, Higher Self. Love, Light, and Chi. As in religious teachings, we make the sign of the cross and say these three names; think of the significance of that gesture. We signify the importance of the crossover to the Union of Love, Light, and Chi. We acknowledge that Love is within and outside. We find a balance in this truth. We find the Divine Union. ❀

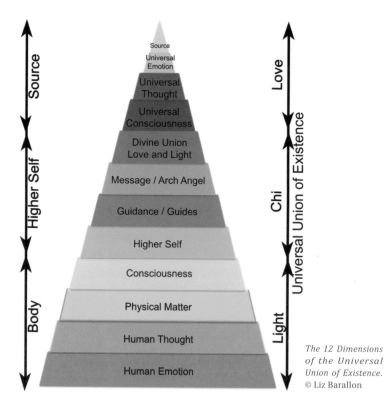

The 12 Dimensions of the Universal Union of Existence. © Liz Barallon

Intention, love, and light.

— LIZ BARALLON —

Chapter 26

THE POWER OF RELEASE

Throughout the book I have given you a structured process to remember every time you need to get your emotions elevated quickly, which is the F.A.S.T.R. Process. For a culture that has been taught to suppress their feelings and to live alone, secluded in their own mind, afraid of judgment and ridicule, it is very hard to expect you, as adults, to know how to control your emotions and actually have the awareness to know when and how to elevate them consciously.

The F.A.S.T.R. Process is designed to help you make elevating to happiness a habit until you no longer need it anymore.

To quickly go through what we have learned so far is important, as this reflection will allow you to realize how far you have come.

F: It is no longer necessary to be afraid to feel your pain. Your pain is there as a gift to help you grow. It is nearly impossible to feel the pain as a gift at the time, but if instead of dwelling in the pain you can look for the lesson, then your ability to grow will increase.

A: Acknowledging and accepting your emotional pain as a lesson is the next step. The ability to write it down to understand the true issue and then take control of your thoughts to lead your emotions to happiness is the key.

S: Starting to take affirmative and constructive action is the next step, and you have been given a series of strategies to help you guide your thoughts, along with the newfound ability to balance and cleanse your energy through meditation and various other energy-healing methods, which will help you reflect on your life choices and how you can grow and change to cross over to happiness.

T: Thanking is the step that comes with the ability to let go. Learning to release the built-up and often-stagnated anger, frustration, and self-guilt will lead you to a place in your journey where you can finally look back at your life, connect all the dots, and see why your journey has led you to this very moment. This is the moment you can say "Thank You" to your past for your present. Because your present is just that. It is a gift!

R: The last stage of the F.A.S.T.R. Process is that of release. I think that as a culture we severely underestimate the power of release. Rather brilliantly, our bodies were actually designed to help release these lower emotions and move up to happiness, but unfortunately, as a whole, we often don't seem to know how to utilize our bodies properly to do this.

CRYING: Crying is the very thing we do when we are faced with the external situation that starts the spiral into the descent of emotional pain. "Boys don't cry." "Big kids don't cry." Yes you do. In fact, you have tear ducts for a reason. The tear duct contains an exocrine gland that is called the lacrimal gland. The lacrimal glands produce tears, and you have three types of tears. The basal tears help keep your eyes lubricated, the reflex tears help flush the eye of any foreign objects or contaminants, and the *psychic* tears are there for you to *release pent up emotions*. Tears even contain a natural painkiller called leucine encephalin.

How good does it feel to have a good cry? How much clearer are your thoughts after you have released your emotions through crying? Crying is the best way to release sadness, clear your thoughts, and move on to the next step. When you cry, your heart rate increases, you sweat, your breathing slows, and you can get a lump in your throat—known as the globus sensation. All these things help release toxins from your body. Some of the *toxins* that you need to eliminate are the *lower emotional energies* your body really doesn't want to keep. This all occurs as a result of your sympathetic nervous system (that's your "fight or flight" system) activating in response to your emotional pain. If you are holding in the tears through pride or guilt, you need to stop doing this *right now*. Pride and guilt are lower emotions, and they only serve the purpose of keeping you stuck in the lower emotions. Allow yourself the kindness of crying because it will help you release so much tension that doesn't belong in your body.

SWEAT: The American College of Sports Medicine states that you sweat not only to cool down when you are hot, but to release toxins and excess salts from your body. You have two types of sweat exocrine glands. You have the eccrine sweat glands, numbered in the millions and located all over your body. They are there to help cool you down. This sweat contains water, sodium, and other substances that cool you as it evaporates off your body.

The other sweat glands are the apocrine glands, and they are found in your armpits and groin. These glands are triggered mostly by your lower emotions. You have probably noticed how stress, anxiety, and worry can get you sweating.

When you exercise, you get hot and you start to sweat. This means that exercising is one of the best releases you can have. Exercise helps release all sorts of feel-good endorphins. These endorphins trigger a positive feeling in the body, similar to that of morphine. This is often described as "euphoric" and can produce a more positive outlook on life. Endorphins also act as analgesics, which means they diminish the perception of pain. They act as sedatives and are manufactured in your brain, spinal cord, and many other parts of your body. These endorphins are released in response to neurotransmitters that are in charge of carrying around your emotional energies. The neuron receptors that endorphins bind to are the same ones that bind some pain medicines.

This is the reason why when you exercise your mind goes into a trancelike state, allowing for reflection on painful matters to occur with more clarity. It is a similar feeling to meditation. It also gives you the added bonus of sweating out the toxins and emotional baggage that you need to release.

ORGASM: I'm not really sure I need to elaborate on this one, but now that I've said it, did you have an aha moment? Yes, an orgasm is one of the biggest releases that can be had, allowing any pent-up emotion to release and become a seriously feel-good moment. How many times have you heard someone who is stressed and under pressure say that they need a good session? During sex, it has been noted that fear and anxiety reduce significantly. The frontal cortex of the brain, which looks after your judgment and moral reasoning, is suppressed. That may explain some of those moments that are quickly regretted the next day. The temporal lobe and the amygdala are also shut down. Importantly, it is the amygdala that has a great deal to do with processing our negative emotions, and, therefore, deactivating the amygdala can lead to a positive emotional influx. The dopamine released during the orgasm also brings with it emotional highs.

Since not everyone orgasms during sex, the act of sex itself is a release, simply because it is the union of love and simply pleasurable to be emotionally bonded with somebody else in such physical and mental closeness.

In saying this, it is not an excuse to become addicted to sex. There is a balance, and the union is always much better with someone you love. Sex can also be a tool for hurting others. So there is a happy balance here, and one that as you ascend in your emotions in the right way, you will come to realize is very important.

WRITE IT DOWN: We have discussed at length how writing down your feelings is a great way to release your pain as you travel slowly through your lower emotions. Even now, as you become clearer in your thoughts and move further up the scale, you can write these little nuances that crop up daily into your gratitude journal in order to release it more quickly. For instance, "I am grateful for the anger I felt today to make me appreciate the calmness I normally enjoy."

SCREAM: Okay, so please try not to scream at someone else, but sometimes when we feel anger that we need to release, the best thing to do is walk into a deserted room or put your face into a pillow and just scream. Screaming can help to release anger and frustration immediately, so that you can approach clarity a little better. It just helps you vibrate the clouds of confusion away so you can see more clearly.

LAUGH, SING, OR DANCE: How much better do you feel when you sing a great song at the top of your lungs or dance around the kitchen while no one is watching. Laughing is always a feel-good release. Music holds a key to our hearts—literally—and makes us feel so many emotions. So put on some great and upbeat music that makes you feel good and get dancing. Because dancing will also increase your sweat, then you will be releasing toxins and producing endorphins as well.

MEDITATION: Meditation, of course, as we have discussed, is a great way to reflect and release lower emotions consciously. Meditation is the ultimate way to receive the clarity you need to move up the emotional scale.

INNER FORGIVENESS: Within the F.A.S.T.R. Process, I talk a lot about reflection. Reflection is about being alone with your thoughts and being able to look back at your life to judge yourself. I have also spoken at lengths about how it is not your place to judge other people, and it is one of the lowest emotions on the scale. But *inner judgment* is a part of reflection. This inner judgment can unfortunately promote self-worthlessness feelings, but once you have reached a certain level of understanding, you will know that true inner judgment isn't about being harsh on yourself. It's about accepting yourself and your limitations and all that makes you who you are. *It's about learning to love what you can't change and change what you can change and deem to need changing.* You can't be good at everything, and you can't feel guilty forever. You need to get to the point where you say, "I have done all that I have done for a reason. That may not have been a good reason at the time, but I am now ready to stop hating myself and start forgiving myself."

Inner forgiveness is the main component of the release needed to move up the scale, and it is like the last key needed to open the door to inner happiness. As I said in the beginning of the book, forgiveness is the toughest emotion to achieve. And that means forgiving yourself for your self-deemed inadequacies. This forgiveness can produce a relief that brings with it a rush of love and acceptance and a true feeling of *letting go.*

Release the pain and set it free for the wind to take away. Accept and love yourself for who you are along with all your faults, and let the light of love carry you over the threshold into the land of happiness. ✺

It's about learning to love what you can't change and change what you can change and deem to need changing.

— LIZ BARALLON —

Chapter 27

THE POWER OF BALANCE

With intentional emotional growth comes an inner happiness and balance in your body that allows your system to work optimally. If you can raise your vibration to be one with love and happiness, then your physical health will follow. Your immune system will work faster and more optimally, your body will utilize its oxygen better, and you will fight off illness easily.

The lonely journey up the emotional scale can ebb and flow like a wave. After the fall into pain your emotions can plummet, but then comes the realization of the truth that you are in control of your own happiness, and you start to feel excited. Then you realize the hard work it takes to heal in a healthy way, and you slip backward again, and then you start to forgive yourself and you feel happy again. It can be a roller coaster of emotions.

I mentioned earlier in the book the unspoken *cycle of inner growth* that I identified to encompass the seven inner steps in every circumstance.

Here they are again to remind you:

Step 1: **to fall**
Step 2: **to realize the truth**
Step 3: **to reflect within**
Step 4: **to forgive**
Step 5: **to embrace**
Step 6: **to love yourself**
Step 7: **to experience joy**

The ebb and flow of emotions. © Liz Barallon

When you go through the spiritual journey and become more in touch with your Higher Self, sometimes it is really easy to become lost in the spiritual side. I find that a lot of my clients will become dissatisfied with general humanity for its lack of awareness. They will become so caught up in the knowledge of the spiritual side of life that they forget to live their physical life, preferring to live in the bliss and elated feeling that comes with knowing your Higher Self and guides more intimately. They forget to come back down to Earth and remain *grounded*.

Balance and harmony are the key to living a happy life. We made a choice to be born into a physical existence in order to experience human connection. Even if you do realize the truth of your inner spirit, it is important to remember that your divine purpose is to experience life. In all of its forms. The good, the bad, and everything in between.

"Contentment" is a word that is seriously underrated. Often the word is associated with boredom. But the definition is actually "a state of happiness and satisfaction." It correlates with the feeling of fulfillment. Contentment is a state of feeling happy with what you have and knowing that you can achieve more whenever you desire. Contentment is the balance that you need to desire. You can go up and down in your emotional state, but you want to aim to vibrate at the frequency of contentment, happiness, and love. The F.A.S.T.R. Process is a habit that will bring you there. ✿

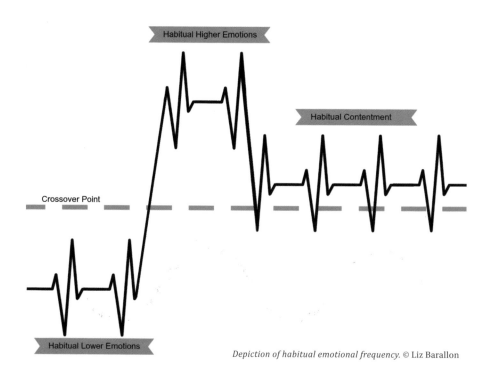

Depiction of habitual emotional frequency. © Liz Barallon

Your divine purpose is to experience life in all of its forms: the good, the bad, and everything in between.

— LIZ BARALLON —

Chapter 28
THE POWER OF HELPING OTHERS

In healing yourself and uplifting your emotions to vibrate at the frequency of happiness or above, you are helping not only yourself, but also all those around you. Simply being a better person and shining your light allows others to resonate at your vibration.

Through increasing your vibration you can affect millions of other people. With the internet at your disposal you can use your light to spread the message of happiness, inspiration, and motivation. You can opt not to get involved in the negativity and, instead, choose a better life decision and accept that which you cannot change to invest in changing your reaction to the external situation.

Your reaction is the only thing within your control. You cannot control others and their thoughts or actions, but you can most certainly control your reaction to the situation. You can choose to invest your time, you can choose to take it personally, you can choose to ignore it, you can choose to not misunderstand, and you can choose to walk away. Ultimately, it is your reaction that will dictate who you become. If you choose to react with understanding, kindness, and love, then you make a difference every time. If you choose to treat others the way you would want to be treated in the same situation, then you can only experience immense inner growth.

The social internet can be a negative echo chamber with lies and mistruths spreading as fast as lightning, and it is disheartening to see such negativity in this time. It is *your responsibility* to uplift yourself. If you want the happiness you deserve, nobody else can do it for you. Your happiness is up to you!

As we discussed earlier in the book, our thoughts operate in coherence within humanity on the large. If we look at the theory that oxygen is the medium for a universal consciousness, and it is capable of uploading our thoughts and emotions and reflecting our desire back to us, then now is the time for everyone to consciously make better choices. Choose to lead with kindness, choose to lead with happiness, and choose to lead with love. Imagine your emotions to be like the disobedient dog that needs puppy school. Your thoughts are the trainer, and you need to teach your emotions to follow you up the emotional scale. Learn to recognize those moments where anger, anxiety, and stress start to resonate, and learn the best release method for you. Work your way up the emotional scale with the F.A.S.T.R. Process and turn it into a habit, and you will easily vibrate at the frequency of happiness and above consistently. You will live in your inner sanctuary.

Once you feel consistently happy and content inside, you will find pleasure in helping others also achieve this happiness. Just to see someone's eyes light up as they realize that they are in control of their lives gives me pure joy. There is no greater satisfaction in life than making a difference to someone else. Most people seem to believe that they have no control over situations that occur to them, and sometimes that is true. But we can always control the way we react to each situation. We can always control our climb back up to happiness. Even in situations where hormones or chemical imbalances happen, these imbalances can be readily changed by following the F.A.S.T.R. methods. Depression is a clinically treatable illness and mostly requires medication. This process will complement the medication and your doctor's advice and allow you to expedite your recovery. Meditation with sound and energy healing is the main complementary therapy that will help with imbalances like these. Consistent chakra cleansing and self-Reiki or professional Reiki treatments will also help you balance your *whole* being.

Is this a method worth spreading? Be proud to share this book with everyone you know. This world needs changing, and maybe, just maybe, this is the message that humanity needs to hear in order to take the first step.

Imagine a world full of people who could healthily deal with their emotions. Imagine a world where parents teach their children that it is okay to cry. Imagine a world where there is a straightforward method for inner happiness that is teachable and workable for each generation. There would be less violence, less bullying, less cruelty, less judgment, and fewer people turning to drugs to numb their emotional pain. There would be more kindness, more happiness, more confidence, and more success. The world's progress would develop a lot faster if more people had the confidence to share their brilliant ideas, and if more people had the self-love to step outside fear and follow their divine light to their divine purpose. ❀

*Be the change
you want to see in the world.*

— MAHATMA GANDHI —

*And be that change coherently,
and watch the world change.*

— LIZ BARALLON —

Chapter 29
THE POWER OF UNDERSTANDING

For the religious, the Bible depicted those who had reached this level of understanding and wisdom with halos of light around their heads.

To put it all into a little bit of perspective, let's highlight the growth stages of the cycle. We awaken, we ascend, and then we are enlightened.

Within this three-step cycle, we go through a seven-step process.

1. We experience the fall.
2. We realize the truth of love.
3. We reflect within.
4. We learn to forgive.
5. We turn and embrace ourselves.
6. We learn to love ourselves.
7. We habitually experience joy.

The power of understanding comes from acknowledging this cycle and understanding the steps we must take to progress through ascension.

The F.A.S.T.R. Process is the five-step process that I have now taught you to use in order to effectively embrace these steps in a healthy way.

Feel

- We must feel the pain from the fall.
- It is important to *feel* your emotions.
- Falling to rock bottom gives you the strength you need to rise again.
- Blocking out the feeling stops you from growing.

Acknowledge

- Acknowledging your pain helps your consciousness take control.
- Emotions are like little puppies that need training.
- It allows you to ask yourself what your version of happiness is.

Start

- We must ask ourselves how to make it better, and put into action a plan to achieve these goals.
- Taking action means using tools to get your headspace in the happy frame of mind.
- Write it down, visualize, meditate, chakra balance, reflect within, decide how to move forward, and actually do it.

Thank

- We must learn that gratitude comes from deep reflection and the ability to thank the external situation.
- Be grateful for the little things.
- Learn to lead your life with love and kindness.
- Always choose the positive thought.
- Thank the pain for allowing you to grow.

Release

- Release the pain by letting go.
- Change what you need to within your control and accept what you can't.
- Cry, sweat it out, write it down, forgive, and release.

Once you have reached the ability to release the pain in a healthy way habitually, then embracing and loving who you are becomes easy. It is the natural progression because you are then doing everything with the best of intentions; you can truly be proud of who you have become, and love all there is to love about you.

Your shine will grow bigger, and the people who meet you will be magnetically attracted to that shine. Those of similar vibration will be attracted to you, and those who are vibrating at a lower level will need to either vibrate up or vibrate out. These are the true lessons in life—to learn your own inner happiness and find the people who boost you up and not bring you down.

Life is about teaching those who want the lessons, and those students will find you when you are ready to teach. Just like you found this book. You felt drawn to something about this book, and you picked it up. Its vibration spoke to your vibration. This book is the teacher you need at this moment.

Awakening is a widely used spiritual and religious term. It encapsulates a lot of different beliefs and opinions, and many different people will give you their version of what they think awakening is. To awaken is just as the word literally says. It is the moment you wake up. The moment you wake up from the reality created for you by other people's beliefs and teachings. It is the moment that you open your third eye and see the truth. This is the truth of who you really are. It is the truth that while you have been busy searching for love externally your whole life, usually being let down, betrayed, and heartbroken, it has been hiding inside all along. The truth is that you cannot feel true love until you look within to find that love for yourself. True love from yourself. It is the truth that your reality is created from your own emotions and thoughts and that you are in fact in the creator of your own reality.

I often find that an awakening in someone usually comes after a period of emotional pain. This is why I associate awakening with the moment you find yourself in the dark of confusion and emotional pain, to then look up and see a glimmer of light shine through.

After you experience your awakening, you then start your ascension. Ascension is translated into "the act of rising to a higher level." This ascension will take your whole life. As humans we choose life so we can learn and experience connection. I don't think that we ever stop learning. Our whole lives are filled with many situations and problems to overcome. Each external influence brings with it a new lesson to learn and a new cycle of falling and rising.

Enlightenment is the moment of self-love. It is the power of knowing that you can get through the tough times. Enlightenment has this definition: "to gain deeper knowledge and understanding about a subject or situation." It means wisdom. Wisdom is the ability to take the knowledge you now have to improve any situation you face. It means the ability to overcome your problems without losing sight of the lesson and the pain. It is the ability to infuse love into every obstacle you encounter, to look for the deeper meaning and the lesson it brings to make you into a better person with an even-greater understanding.

Let me tell you about a number. The number 1000 is the last individually named Hebrew number. It is thought to mean the completion of the cycle. There is much debate on the meanings of the Hebrew numbers, but I have spent a lot of time studying these numbers and their meanings. The number 1000 in Hebrew is א׳, and it is sounded as Eleph. El, as we have discussed, translates into the word "love." Eph translates into "risen." The word *Eleph* means "risen in love."

When you think of an elephant, you can visualize an elephant trunk rising. An elephant has also been associated with wisdom, and most ethologists view the elephant as the world's most intelligent animal. Aristotle described the elephant as "the animal that surpasses all others in wit and mind." Elephants have a very large hippocampus, which is much bigger than humans'. The hippocampus is the area of the brain that has emotional memory. Elephants also show empathy for other animals and will help different animals in need. This is a sign of an enlightened being. The word "elephant" literally denotes the action of being risen in love.

It brings another meaning to the white elephant in the room that we spoke of in the second chapter. No longer can you ignore him, but you must acknowledge and embrace the white elephant into your life and push forward with accomplishing your dreams.

1000 is a number that completes a cycle. It is a powerful number that shows the growth of the cycle of awaken, ascend, and enlighten. To reach 1000, it is said you have become the creator of your own reality. You are now able to reflect your external reality to mirror your new and improved inner environment.

1000 is our completion of the cycle of the F.A.S.T.R. Process. It is a feeling of knowing that with this new tool, you can overcome any obstacle. You can overcome any ingrained belief about yourself and choose to find the way forward.

You now have the power of balance, harmony, and love, and you can use it not only to improve your own health and vitality but to improve humanity one step at a time. *Waking up in the darkness is just the start.*

Love and Light,
Liz Barallon

Liz Barallon *is a life coach, energy healer, and mum to three girls from sunny Queensland, Australia. Having run a successful business in network marketing, Liz found a love for helping her team members realize their own goals and dreams through teaching them to face their fears and understand their own self-worth. She decided to pursue this passion further and went on to study life coaching, energy healing, and vibrational medicine. Through combining these modalities in her business, Start Your Life Abundance, she was able to incorporate a holistic way to help her clients focus on the energetic output of their emotions in order to help them manifest their desired reality. For more information about Liz, her teachings, and the products she recommends, please visit her website: www.stresstohappy.com.*

Bibliography

Abarim Publications: Patterns in the Bible. Abarim Publications, last updated November 2017. www.abarim-publications.com.

Armour, J. Andrew, David A. Murphy, Bing-Xiang Yuan, Sara MacDonald, and David A. Hopkins. "Gross and Microscopic Anatomy of the Human Intrinsic Cardiac Nervous System." *Anatomical Record* 247, no. 2 (1997): 289–298. https://onlinelibrary.wiley.com/doi/full/10.1002/%28SICI%291097-0185%28199702%29247%3A2%3C289%3A%3AAID-AR15%3E3.0.CO%3B2-L.

Baudel, Jerome. Reiki Healer 1. Course, Ashati Institute, 2016. www.ashati.org.

The Bible: New International Version. Bible Study Tools, 2018. www.biblestudytools.com.

Braden, Gregg. "Physics of Our Deepest Connections." *Missing Links with Gregg Braden*. Gaia TV, season 1, episode 6, February 2, 2017.

Braden, Gregg. *The Divine Matrix: Bridging Time, Space, Miracles and Belief*. New Delhi: Hay House, 2007.

Buks, Eyal, Ralph Schuster, Mordehai Heiblum, Diana Mahalu, and Vladimir Umansky. "Dephasing in Electron Interference by a 'Which-Path' Detector." *Science Daily*, 391, no. 6670 (February 27, 1998): 871–74.

Butusov, Mikhail, and Arne Jernelöv. *Phosphorus: An Element That Could Have Been Called Lucifer*. New York: Springer, 2013.

Castro, Giovanna. "Emotional Climax." *Emotion of the Brain* (blog), October 24, 2014. http://sites.tufts.edu/emotiononthebrain/2014/10/24/emotional-climax/.

Cruz, Renae. "Renae Cruz Spiritual Guidance." *SolAwakening* (blog). Last updated May 10, 2018. www.solawakening.com.

Docter, Pete, dir. *Inside Out*. Original story by Pete Docter and Ronnie del Carmen. DVD. Emeryville, CA: Disney, 2015.

Emoto, Masaru. *The True Power of Water: Healing and Discovering Ourselves*. New York: Atria Books, 2005. www.masaru-emoto.net.

Fiorenza, N. A. "Planetary Harmonics & Neurobiological Resonances in Light, Sound, & Brain Wave Frequencies: Including the Translation of Sound to Color." Lunar Planner, 2003–2017. www.lunarplanner.com.

Ford, G. "Life Coach Training Program." Diploma, Health & Harmony Colleges, 2015. www.healthandharmony.com.au.

Ford, G. "Vibrational Medicine." Diploma, Health & Harmony Colleges, 2015. www.healthandharmony.com.au.

Fosar, Grażyna, and Franz Bludorf. *Vernetzte Intelligenz*. 2nd ed. Aachen, Germany: Omega, 2003.

Gariaev, P. P., and Vladimir Poponin. "Vacuum DNA Phantom Effect In Vitro and Its Possible Rational Explanation." *Nanobiology* (1995): 11–12.

Google Dictionary. www.google.com.au/search?q=Dictionary.

Google Translate. https://translate.google.com.au/.

Hagelin, John S. "Is Consciousness the Unified Field? A Field Theorist's Perspective." Maharishi International University, Fairfield, IA. www.mum.edu/wp-content/uploads/2014/07/hagelin.pdf.

Hagelin, John. *Restructuring Physics from Its Foundations in Light of Maharishi Vedic Science*. Fairfield, IA: Maharishi University of Management Press, 1989.

Hansen, Julieann. "The Science of Sweat." *American College of Sports Medicine* (blog), May 21, 2013. www.certification.acsm.org/blog/2013/may/the-science-of-sweat.

HeartMath Institute. HeartMath Institute Research Library. Last updated 2018. www.heartmath.org/research/research-library.

Hicks, Jerry, and Esther Hicks. *Ask and It Is Given: Learning to Manifest Your Desires*. Carlsbad, CA: Hay House, 2004. www.AbrahamHicks.com.

Horowitz, Leonard G. *The Book of 528: Prosperity Key of LOVE*. Las Vegas, NV: Tetrahedron, 2018.

Horowitz, Leonard G., and Joseph Puleo. *Healing Codes for the Biological Apocalypse*. Sandpoint, ID: Tetrahedron, 1999.

Hulse, David. "About the Ancient Solfeggio Frequencies." *Somaenergetics* (blog), 2016a. www.somaenergetics.com/pages/ancient-solfeggio-frequencies.

Hulse, David. "Forgotten in Time: The Ancient Solfeggio Frequencies." *Somaenergetics* (blog), 2016b. www.somaenergetics.com/pages/forgotten-in-time-the-ancient-solfeggio-frequencies.

Kar. "Attuned Vibrations." Attuned Vibrations, 2016. www.attunedvibrations.com.

Keyes, Ken, Jr. *Handbook to Higher Consciousness*. 5th ed. Berkeley, CA: Living Love Center, 1993.

Knight, Nick. "Why Do We Cry? The Science of Tears." *Independent* (blog), September 18, 2014. www.independent.co.uk/life-style/health-and-families/features/why-do-we-cry-the-science-of-tears-9741287.html.

Kosslyn, Stephen M., and G. Wayne Miller. *Top Brain, Bottom Brain: Surprising Insights into How You Think*. New York: Simon & Schuster, 2013.

LeMind, Anna. "The Universe May Have a Consciousness of Its Own, Say Scientists." *The Mind Unleashed: Uncover Your True Potential* (blog), July 5, 2017. https://themindunleashed.com/2017/07/universe-consciousness.html.

Luskin, Fred. "What Is Forgiveness?" *Greater Good Magazine* (blog), August 19, 2010. https://greatergood.berkeley.edu/topic/forgiveness/definition#what-is.

Majors, Charles, Ben Lerner, and Sayer Ji. *Cancer Killers (the Cause Is the Cure)*. Orlando, FL: Maximized Living, 2013.

Mascaro, Juan. *The Dhammapada*. London: Penguin Books, 1973.

Mercola, Joseph. "Modern Research Reveals Your Heart Does Have a Mind of Its Own." *Take Control of Your Health* (blog), March 5, 2016. https://articles.mercola.com/sites/articles/archive/2016/03/05/brain-heart-emotion.aspx.

"Midi-chlorian." *Wookieepedia, the* Star Wars *Wiki* (blog). Last updated May 2018. www.starwars.wikia.com/wiki/Midi-chlorian.

NERIS Analytics Limited. "16 Personalities." NERIS Analytics Limited, 2013–2018. www.16personalities.com.

"Our Conscious Mind Could Be an Electromagnetic Field." *Daily University Science News*, May 16, 2002. www.unisci.com/stories/20022/0516026.htm.

Ramsey, Peter, dir. *Rise of the Guardians*. Hollywood, CA: DreamWorks, 2012. Based on the book *The Guardians of Childhood* by William Joyce (New York: Simon & Schuster, 2015).

Rein, Glen. "Biological Effects of Scalar Acoustic Energy." Paper presented at the annual conference of the US Psychotronics Association, held in July 1998 in Columbus, OH.

Rein, Glen. "Effect of Conscious Intention on Human DNA." Paper presented at the International Forum on New Science held in October 1996 in Denver, CO. www.item-bioenergy.com/infocenter/consciousintentionondna.pdf.

Rein, Glen. "Storage of Non-Hertzian Frequency Information in Water." *Innovative Biophysical Technologies* (blog). Last updated 2018. www.innobioteck.com/water-research.html.

Rein, Glen, and Rolin McCraty. "Structural Changes of Water and DNA Associated with New Physiologically Measurable States." *Journal of Scientific Exploration* 8, no. 3 (1994): 438–39.

Richardson, Alan. "Mental Practice: A Review and Discussion Part I." *Research Quarterly: American Association for Health, Physical Education and Recreation* 38, no. 1 (1967): 95–107.

Richardson, Alan. "Mental Practice: A Review and Discussion Part II." *Research Quarterly: American Association for Health, Physical Education and Recreation* 38, no. 2 (1967): 263–73.

Rosie. "Pyramids as Resonant Sound Chambers." *Wholistic Sound* (blog), September 2, 2013. www.wholisticsound.blogspot.com.au/2013/09/pyramids-as-resonant-sound-chambers.html.

Rouse, Margaret. "Unified Field Theory or Theory of Everything (TOE)." *Tech Target* (blog). Last updated 2005. http://whatis.techtarget.com/definition/unified-field-theory-or-Theory-of-Everything-TOE.

Scaccia, Annamarya. "Serotonin: What You Need to Know." Medically reviewed by Debra Rose Wilson, PhD. *Healthline Media*, May 18, 2017. www.healthline.com/health/mental-health/serotonin.

Scripture4all Foundation. "Hebrew Interlinear Bible (OT)." Scripture4all Foundation, 2008. www.scripture4all.org.

Sheldon, Christie. "Love or Above." Course, Mind Valley Institute, Kuala Lumpur, 2015.

Shoshanna, Brenda. *Zen and the Art of Falling in Love*. New York: Simon & Schuster, 2004.

Tesla, Nikola. "The Transmission of Electrical Energy without Wires as a Means for Furthering Peace." *Electrical World and Engineer* 45 (January 7, 1905): 21–24. www.tfcbooks.com/tesla/1905-01-07.htm.

TMHome. "Unified Field of Consciousness: ONE = MANY." *Transcendental Meditation* (blog). Last modified July 15, 2013. www.tmhome.com/news-events/unified-field-of-consciousness-onemany.

van Lommel, Pim. *Consciousness beyond Life: The Science of the Near-Death Experience.* New York: HarperOne, 2010.

van Lommel, Pim, Ruud van Wees, Vincent Meyers, and Ingrid Elfferich. "Near-Death Experience in Survivors of Cardiac Arrest: A Prospective Study in the Netherlands." *The Lancet,* December 15, 2001. www.thelancet.com/journals/lancet/article/PIIS0140673601071008/fulltext.

Vithoulkas, George, and Dafin F. Muresanu. "Conscience and Consciousness: A Definition." *Journal of Medicine and Life* 7, no. 1 (2014): 104–108.

Wilde, Dana. *Train Your Brain.* Bloomington, IN: Balboa, 2013.

Wurtman, Judith J., and Nina T. Frusztajer. *The Serotonin Power Diet: Eat Carbs—Nature's Own Appetite Suppressant—to Stop Emotional Overeating and Halt Antidepressant-Associated Weight Gain.* Emmaus, PA: Rodale Books, 2010.

Yue, Guang, and Kelly J. Cole. "Strength Increases from the Motor Program: Comparison of Training with Maximal Voluntary and Imagined Muscle Contractions." *Journal of Neurophysiology* 67, no. 5 (1992): 1114–23.

ACKNOWLEDGMENTS

Through the years of research I have done and information I have gained, I wanted to make a few special mentions to people whose work may or may not be referenced directly within the book but is infused into my knowledge and opinions. I would like to thank Dana Wilde for being my first online coach and mentor regarding her fabulous work in the networking industry, and her course and book by the same name, *Train Your Brain*. Dana's work has really been a huge influence on my style, and I absolutely recommend her work wholeheartedly. I would like to thank the Ashati Institute for all your help with my lessons in Reiki and assistance in developing my love of this fantastic modality.

I would also like to thank the Health & Harmony Colleges in Australia for helping me gain my diplomas in life coaching and vibrational medicine. I took twice as long to finish my diploma because the information contained within the course sparked my interest in so many fields that I ended up on hourlong tangents on a daily basis.

I would like to thank Hiro Emoto for your prompt, courteous, and diligent manner in helping me gain the rights to use Dr. Emoto's images in this book.

I would like to thank Warren Scheidel for taking several hours out of his day to take photos of flowers and fauna for me. www.facebook.com/waza81shotz

I would also like to thank Maria and Veronica for helping to create a wonderful headshot.

Thank you also to my friend Jayne for reading my book in its earliest stages.

Thank you to Dinah for seeing the power of my manuscript and giving me the opportunity to publish my book.

And last, thank you to my family for allowing me to place my life on hold for a little while so I could finish the book.